PROGRAMMING A PROBLEM-ORIENTED LANGUAGE

Charles H. Moore
written ~ June 1970

Preface

This is an unpublished book I wrote long ago. Just after I'd written the first versions of Forth. Perhaps it explains the motivation behind Forth. There is some interest in it, and publishing is no longer relevant since I can post it on my website.
I have a typescript that I recovered from Forth, Inc long ago. I had typed it on my Smith-Corona portable, complete with overstrikes and annotations. It is illegible enough to discourage a casual reader, so I'm re-keying it in HTML.
This is useful, since I used to be a good typist and that skill has deteriorated. My fingers can use the exercise and I'm curious if I can reduce my error rate.
I'm making minimal changes to the text; just enough to fit HTML. The language remains quaint, ungrammatical or unclear. Any remaining typos are modern.

Chuck Moore 2011
COMPUTER DIVISION
File Copy

The information in his eBook has been collected from different sources, edited, formatted and prepared for eBook publication in appreciation for all the good work Charles did for designers.
Very little has been changed to leave it as original as possible.
Charles agreed to have it published as eBook and as printed book.

Juergen Pintaske, ExMark, 29 April 2014. Published as print v8 July 2018

This Book is Copyright © ExMark, 08 July 2018
And part of the current amazon Forth Bookshelf to be found at
https://www.amazon.co.uk/Juergen-Pintaske/e/B00N8HVEZM

1 **Charles Moore** - Forth - The Early Years: Background information about the beginnings of this Computer Language

2 **Charles Moore** - Programming A Problem Oriented Language: Forth - how the internals work - **Now as eBook and as print book**

3 **Leo Brodie** - Starting Forth, the classic

4 **Leo Wong / Juergen Pintaske / Stephen Pelc** FORTH LITE TUTORIAL: Code tested with MPE VFX Forth, SwiftForth and Gforth

5 **Juergen Pintaske – A START WITH FORTH** – Article Collection – 12 Words to start, then 35 Words, Javascript Forth, and much more

6 **Stephen Pelc** - Programming Forth: Version July 2016

7 **Tim Hentlass** - Real Time Forth

8 **Brad Rodriguez** - Moving Forth / TTL CPU / B.Y.O. Assembler

9 **Chen-Hanson Ting** - Footsteps In An Empty Valley issue 3

10 **Chen-Hanson Ting** - Zen and the Forth Language: EFORTH for the MSP430G2552 from Texas Instruments

11 **Chen-Hanson Ting** - eForth and Zen - 3rd Edition 2017: with 32-bit 86eForth v5.2 for Visual Studio 2015

12 **Chen-Hanson Ting** - eForth Overview

13 **Chen-Hanson Ting** - FIG-Forth Manual and Test on FPGA 1802

14 **Chen-Hanson Ting** - EP32 RISC Processor IP: Description and Implementation into FPGA – ASIC tested by NASA

15 **Chen-Hanson Ting** – Irriducible Complexity

16 **Burkhard Kainka** - Learning Programming with MyCo: Learning Programming easily – PC independent (Forth code to follow soon)

17 **Burkhard Kainka** - BBC Micro:bit: Tests Tricks Secrets Code, Additional MicroBit information when running the Mecrisp Package

18 **Burkhard Kainka&Thomas Baum** – Sparrow Programs, TINY13

Contents

Chapter 1	Introduction	6
1.1	The Basic Principle	8
1.2	Preview	12
Chapter 2	Programs without input	15
2.1	Choosing a language	17
2.2	Choosing a computer	21
2.3	Arrangement and formatting	22
2.4	Mnemonics	24
2.5	Routines and subroutines	26
Chapter 3	Programs with input	28
3.1	Nouns and verbs	29
3.2	Control loop	35
3.3	Word subroutine	38
3.3.1	Message I/O	40
3.3.2	Moving characters	42
3.4	Decimal conversion	44
3.4.1	Numbers	45
3.4.2	Input conversion	50
3.4.3	Output conversion	53
3.5	Stacks	56
3.5.1	Return stack	57
3.5.2	Parameter stack	58
3.6	Dictionary	60
3.6.1	Entry format	61
3.6.2	Search strategies	64
3.6.3	Initialization	66
3.7	Control language - an example	67
Chapter 4	Programs that grow	69
4.1	Adding dictionary entries	71
4.2	Deleting entries	74

4.3	Operations	76
4.4	Definition entries	80
4.4.1	Definition	84
4.4.2	Execution	88
4.4.3	Conditions	91
4.4.4	Loops	96
4.4.5	Implementation	99
4.5	Code entries	103
Chapter 5	Programs with memory	108
5.1	Organization of disk	109
5.1.1	Getting blocks	110
5.1.2	Releasing blocks	112
5.1.3	Reading and writing	113
5.2	Text on disk	115
5.2.1	Text editing	117
Chapter 6	Programs with output	120
6.1	Output routines	122
6.2	Acknowledgement	123
6.3	Character strings	126
6.4	Field entries	129
Chapter 7	Programs that share	131
7.0.1	Non-user activities	133
7.0.2	Message handling	135
7.1	User control	136
7.2	Queing	138
7.2.1	Usage	141
7.3	Private dictionaries	142
7.3.1	Memory protection	143
7.3.2	Controlled access	145
7.4	Disk buffers	146
7.5	User swapping	147
Chapter 8	Programs that think	149

8.1	Word dissection	150
8.2	Level definitions	154
8.3	Infinite dictionary	162
8.4	Infinite memory	167
Chapter 9	Programs that bootstrap	172
9.1	Getting started	174
9.2	The roots	176
9.3	The branches	178
Pictures A	Figure 1, 2, 3	180
Picture B	Figure 6.2	181
The Author	Charles H Moore	

1. Introduction

I'm not sure why you're reading this book. It's taken me a while to discover why I'm writing it. Let's examine the title: *Programming a Problem-Oriented-Language*. The key word is programming. I've written many programs over the years. I've tried to write *good* programs, and I've observed the manner in which I write them rather critically. My goal has been to decrease the effort required and increase the quality produced.

In the course of these observations, I've found myself making the same mistakes repeatedly. Mistakes that are obvious in retrospect, but difficult to recognise in context. I thought that if I wrote a prescription for programming, I could at least remind myself of problems. And if the result is of value to me, it should be of value to others; if what I say is new to you, you may learn something of value; if I cover familiar ground, you at least get a new point of view.

I've also been distressed at the lack of concern from others about problems I consider significant. It amounts to a general indifference to quality; a casual attitude of confidence that one's programs are pretty good, in any case as good as necessary. I'm convinced this confidence is misplaced. Moreover, this attitude is reinforced by the massive trend to high-level languages and a placid acceptance of their inefficiencies: What's the use of designing a really good algorithm if the compiler's going to botch it up anyway?

So, I've written a book about programming. I have no great taste for debating over a one-way communication link and no real interest in convincing you that I'm right in what I say. So, you'll probably find that I'm being brusk. I'm quite likely to state bluntly something you may take issue with. Please do! My intention is to document an approach I've found useful, and perhaps to stimulate critical interest in programming. If you care enough to take issue, I'm delighted.

Back to the title. What about Problem-Oriented-Language? I didn't start out to write about that; and I'm not sure that I'm qualified to do so. But I discovered that in order to justify what I was doing and identify the appropriate circumstances for doing it, the term became essential.

A problem-oriented-language is a language tailored to a particular application. To avoid that uniquely clumsy term, I'll usually substitute *application language* as synonymous. Very often such a language isn't recognised for what it is. For instance, if your program reads a code in column 80 to identify an input card, you are implementing an application language. A very crude one, a very awkward one; mostly because you hadn't given the matter any thought. Recognising the problem, I'm sure you can design a better solution. This book will show you how.

1.1 The Basic Principle

We have a large number of subjects to talk about. I'm going to throw before you a lot of techniques that you may be able to use. This is basically the result of the nature of a digital computer: a general-purpose tool for processing information.

A computer can do anything. I hope that you realize that, providing you allow me to define "anything", I can prove this. I mean real, incontrovertible, mathematical-type proof. A computer cannot do everything. I can prove this, too. But most important, with only you and I to program it, a computer cannot even do very much. This is of the nature of an empirical discovery.

So to offer guidance when the trade-offs become obscure, I am going to define the Basic Principle:

Keep it Simple

As the number of capabilities you add to a program increases, the complexity of the program increases exponentially. The problem of maintaining compatibility among these capabililties, to say nothing of some sort of internal consistency in the program, can easily get out of hand. You can avoid this if you apply the Basic Principle. You may be acquainted with an operating system that ignored the Basic Principle.

It is very hard to apply. All the pressures, internal and external, conspire to add features to your program. After all, it only takes a half-dozen instructions; so why not? The only opposing pressure is the Basic Principle, and if you ignore it, there is no opposing pressure.

In order to help you apply the Basic Principle, I'm going to tell you how many instructions you should use in some routines. And how large a program with certain capabilities should be. These numbers are largely machine independent; basically, they measure the complexity of the task. They are based upon routines I have used in my programs, so I can substantiate them. Let me warn you now that I'll be talking about programs that will fit comfortably in 4K words of core.

The Basic Principle has a corollary:

Do Not Speculate!

Do not put code in your program that *might* be used. Do not leave hooks on which you can hang extensions. The things you might want to do are infinite; that means that each one has 0 probability of realization. If you need an extension later, you can code it later - and probably do a better job than if you did it now. And if someone else adds the extension, will they notice the hooks you left? Will you document that aspect of your program?

The Basic Principle has another corollary:

Do It Yourself!

Now we get down the the nitty-gritty. This is our first clash with the establishment. The conventionsl approach, enforced to a greater or lesser extent, is that you shall use a standard subroutine. I say that you should write your own subroutines.

Before you can write your own subroutine, you have to know how. This means, to be practical, that you have written it before; which makes it difficult to get started. But give it a try. After writing the same subroutine a dozen times on as many computers and languages, you'll be pretty good at it. If you don't plan to be programming that long, you won't be interested in this book.

What sort of subroutines do you write for yourself? I have acquired respect for SQRT subroutines. They're tricky things; seem to attract a lot of talent. You can use the library routine to good advantage. Input subroutines now. They seem to have crawled out from under a rock. I somehow can't agree that the last word was said 15 years ago when FORMAT statements were invented.

As I will detail later, the input routine is the most important code in your program. After all, no one sees your program; but everyone sees your input. To abdicate to a system subroutine that hasn't the slightest interest in your particular problem is foolish. The same can be said for output subroutine and disk-access subroutine.

Moreovere, the task is not that great as to deter you. Although it takes hundreds of instructions to write a general-purpose subroutine, you can do what you need with tens of instructions. In fact, I would advise against writing a subroutine longer that a hundred instructions.

So, if you want to read double-precision, complex integers; don't rely on the COBOL input subroutine or wait till the manufacturer revises it. It's a lot easier to write your own.

But suppose everyone wrote their own subroutines? Isn't that a step backward; away from the millenium when our programs are machine independent, when we all write in the same language, maybe even on the same computer? Let me take a stand: I can't solve the problems of the world. With luck, I can write a good program.

1.2 Preview

I'm going to tell you how to write a program. It is a specific program; that is, a program with a specific structure and capabilities. In particular, it is a program that can be expanded from simple to complex along a well-defined path, to handle a wide range of problems, likewise varying from simple to complex. One of the problems it considers is exactly the problem of complexity. How can you control your program so that it doesn't grow more complicated than your application warrants?

First, I'll define "input", and mention some general rules of programming that apply to all programs, whether they have input or not. Actually, we will be almost exclusively concerned with input, so I've not much to say about programs lacking input.

By admitting input, a program acquires a control language by which a user can guide the program through a maze of possibilities. Naturally, this increases the flexibility of the program, it also requires a more complex application to justify it. However, it is possible to achieve a considerable simplification of the program, by recognising that it needs a control language as a tool of implementation.

The next step is a problem-oriented-language. By permitting the program to dynamically modify its control language, we mark a qualitative change in capability. We also change our attention from the program to the language it implements. This is an important, and dangerous, diversion. For it's easy to lose sight of the problem amidst the beauty of the solution.

In a sense, our program has evolved into a meta-language, which describes a language we apply to the application. But having mentioned meta-language, I want to explain why I won't use the term again. You see things get pretty complicated, particularly on a philosophic level. To precisely describe our situation requires not 2 levels of language - language and meta-language - but a least 4 levels. To distinguish between these levels requires subtle arguments that promote not clarity but confusion. Moreover, the various levels can often be interchanged in practice, which reduces the philosophic arguments to hair-splitting.

A problem-oriented-language can express any problem I've encountered. And remember, we're not concerned with the language, but with the program that makes the language work. By modifying the language, we can apply the same program to many applications. However, there are a class of extensions to the language that constitute another qualitative change. They don't increase the capacity of the program, but they increase the capability of the language. That is, they make the language more expressive. We will consider some such extensions in Chapter 8. I gathered them together chiefly because they share the common property that I don't quite comprehend their potential. For example, I think the language applies the concepts of English.

Finally, I want to describe a process whereby you can implement this program in machine language. That is, a bootstrap technique whereby a basic program can modify and expand itself.

I hope you find the ideas I describe of value to you. In particular, I hope that you will agree that the program I describe has a certain inevitability; that it must do certain things, it must do them in a certain order, and that a certain set of conventions yield an optimal solution.

I've gone to some lengths to simplify. I hope that you don't find too many violations of the Basic Principle, for it's much easier to elaborate upon a program than it is to strip it to basics. You should feel free to build upon my basic routines, provided that you recognise that you are adding a convenience. If you confuse what is expedient with what is necessary, I guarantee your program will never stop growing.

You will notice a lack of flow-charts. I've never liked them, for they seem to include a useless amount of information - either too little or too much. Besides they imply a greater rigidity in program structure than usually exists. I will be quite specific about what I think you should do and how you should do it. But I will use words, and not diagrams. I doubt that you would give a diagram the attention it deserved, anyway. Or that I would in preparing it.

2. Programs without input

The simplest possible program is one that has no input. That is a somewhat foolish statement, but if you'll give me a chance to explain we can establish some useful definitions.
First consider the word "input". I want to use it in a specific sense:

Input is information that controls a program.

In particular, I do not consider as input:

Moving data between media within the computer. For instance, copying tape onto disk, or disk into core.

Reading data into the computer. This is really a transfer between media:
from card to core.

However, data very often has input mixed with it - information that identifies or disposes of the data. For example, a code in col. 80 might identify a card. It is input, the rest of the card probably data.

Many programs have input of a kind I shall disregard: operating systems use control cards to specify which files to assign, which subroutines to collect, etc. Such information is definitely input to the operating system. Although it may affect the operation of your program, ignore it because it is not under your control - unless your program is the operating system itself.

In order to sharpen your recognition of input, let me describe a program that has input. Consider a program that fits a smooth curve through measured data points. It needs a lot of information in order to run: the number of data points, the spacing between points, the number of iterations to perform, perhaps even which function to fit. This information might be built into the program; if it is not, it must be supplied as input. The measured data itself, the object of the entire program, is not input; but must be accompanied by input in order to to intelligible.

A program that has no input may be extremely complex. Lacking input simply means the program knows what to do without being told. That built into the code is all the information needed to run. If you are willing to re-compile the program, you can even modify it without input.

But I'll be viewing programs from the input side. I'll be ranking programs according to the complexity of their input and I plan to demonstrate that a modest increase in the complexity of input can provide a substantial decrease in the complexity of the program. From this point of view, a program with no input is simple.

Since I'm going to be talking about input, a program without input it leaves me nothing to talk about. But I want to make some points about programs in general, so I'll make them here. For one thing, we will be climbing a tree. When we reach the higher branches we'll have enough trouble keeping our balance without worrying about the roots.

2.1 Choosing a language

We shall be less interested in computer language than most programmers. For 3 reasons: First, we will eventually define our own application-oriented language. How we implement that language is of lesser concern. Second, you probably aren't in a position to pick a language. Your installation probably has reduced your choice to nil. Third, we won't be talking about problems at the language level.

This last comment deserves elaboration. I assume that you are already a competent programmer. I'm not interested in teaching you how a computer works, or how a language conceals the computer. I want to talk about problems common to all programs in a machine-independent and language-independent manner. I will leave to you the details of implementation. I am not going to write a program, I am going to show you how to write a program.

I hope that you are a good enough programmer to think in computerese. That is, as someone discusses their application, you interpret it in terms of computer operations: a loop here, a calculation there, a decision . . . The details are largely irrelevant, the gross structure of the program is of concern.

As you put more thought into the problem, you begin to relate it to your particular machine: this data comes off tape, that loop is stopped by . . ., this is really a 3-way branch. you modify the problem as required by your particular hardware configuration.

Finally, you must translate your program into a particular language. You encounter a new class of problem: your FORTRAN won't run that loop backwards, COBOL doesn't have a 3-way branch, you couldn't access the data that way... Current languages put more constraints on this last coding process than they should.

I'll have a bit more to say about languages, but mostly we'll stay at the most abstract level - talking computerese. We won't be talking in meta-language exclusively. I may tell you to load an index-register or to jump on negative and you'll have to translate that into the equivalent for your computer and language.

Now let's look at the major failing of higher-level languages. In attempting to achieve machine-independence and to be applicable to a wide range of applications, they only give you acess to a fraction of the capabilities of your computer. If you compare the number of loop control instructions on your computer to the number of loop constructs in your language, you'll see what I mean.

Let me indulge in a 1-sentence characterization of 3 popular languages to illustrate their restricted capabilities:

FORTRAN is great at evaluating complicated algebraic expressions.

COBOL is great at processing packed decimal data.

ALGOL is great at providing loops and conditional statements.

Each language can be very efficient at its sort of job. But if you want conditional loops involving complicated decimal expressions you have a problem.

We are going to be concerned with efficiency. We are going to do some things that if we don't do efficiently, we can't do at all. Most

of these things will not fit in the framework of a higher-level
language. Some will; others will demand controlled use of the
hardware that a compiler doesn't permit. For example, upon
entering a FORTRAN subroutine it may save the registers it uses. If
you didn't need to save them you've wasted time and space. An
ALGOL subroutine may expect registers available that you have
reserved; then you have to save them. It may well cost you more
effort to interface with the compiler than it saves you in return.

Moreover, none of these languages are very good at moving things
around. Most statements are data transfers - count them in your
latest program. There is a profound philosophical truth concealed in
how much we can accomplish by moving numbers around. If we
can move several things with one instruction or put the same
register several places - we can't afford not to.

You will have to code in assembler! Not the whole program, if you
insist, but the important parts that we'll be concentrating on. You
might be able to do some of these in FORTRAN, but it simply isn't
worth the effort. I'll show you where higher-level subroutines can
go, and I think you'll agree there is good reason to restrict them to
that function.

I recognise the drawbacks of assembler and chafe at them as much
as anyone. I don't like to punch and debug 10 times as many cards
either. But I will in order to get the performance I need. By the way,
I will use the word "compiler" to include assembler; we will *compile*
an assembly language program.

Later I'll show you how to write a program in a forgotten language:
machine language. By that I mean sitting at the console and
entering absolute, binary instructions with the switches. Depending

on the hardware and software available, and the nature of your application, it may just be the best language of all.

2.2 Choosing a computer

Of course I don't expect that you're in a position to choose a computer. Nor am I going to discuss hardware at all. But I do have a mental image of the kind of computer, and explaining it may help you understand some of my comments.

Most applications can be programmed very nicely on a small computer: say 4K of 16-bit words with a typical instruction set, floating-point hardware if needed. If, that is so, the computer is augmented with random access secondary memory, which I will call disk. The capacity of disk is unimportant, even a small disk providing plenty for our purposes, and is determined by the application. However, it is important to be able to copy the disk onto another disk, or tape, for back-up. Thus, I envisage a small computer with 2 secondary memories, and of course a keyboard or card-reader and printer or scope for input and output.

Instead of running applications in serial on a small computer, you can run them in parallel on a large one. I see no advantage, for the amount of core and disk you can afford to use for a single application is about that available on a small computer. You don't gain speed, you suffer from a complex operating system, and you have a enormous capital investment. But the configuration I have in mind remains the same: 4K of core, secondary memory and input/output device.

2.3 Arrangement and formatting

Now I'm going to tell you how to write a program, independent of language or computer. Things you ought to be doing already, but probably aren't because noone ever told you to. Little things. but if you don't do them you won't have a good program; and we're going to write a good program.

Remember the Basic Principle! If you didn't read the Introduction, do it now.

Declare all variables. Even in FORTRAN when you don't have to. Everyone likes to know what parameters you are using, presumably need to use; likes to count them, to see if they could use fewer; is annoyed if you slip one in without mentioning it.

Define everything you can before you reference it. Even in FORTRAN when you don't have to. Why not? You don't like to read a program backwards either. 'Everything you can' means everything except forward jumps. You better not have many forward jumps.

Make the variables as GLOBAL as possible. Why not? You can save some space and clarify your requirements. For instance, how many Is, Js and Ks do you need? In most cases a single copy in COMMON would suffice (you have to declare them, remember, and may as well put them in COMMON); you can redefine it locally if you must; and it is of interest that you must.

Indent! High-level languages, even modern assemblers, fail to insist that you start in column x. But you do! The unbelievable appeal of a straight left margin! Paper is 2-dimensional. Use it! If you indent all statements inside a loop, it's obvious at a glance the extent of the loop. If you indent conditionally executed statements, you'll find that nested conditions sort themselves out - automatically. If you indent little statements you wish you didn't have to include (I = I) you'll find they intrude less as you glance through the listing. Always indent the same amount, 3 spaces/level is good. Be consistant and be accurate. Sloppy indenting is obvious.

2.4 Mnemonics

You will find as you read, that I have strong opinions on some subjects and no opinion of others. Actually, I have strong opinions on all, but sometimes I can't make up my mind which to express. Fortunately, it leaves you some decisions to make for yourself.

Use words with mnemonic value. Unfortunately, what is mnemonic to you may not be mnemonic to me; and I'm the one who judges. Also, unfortunately, mnemonic words tend to be long, which conflicts with:

Use short words. You don't want to type long words, and I don't want to read them. In COBOL this means avoid dashes and avoid qualification, though both can be useful upon occasion.

So, let me suggest a compromise: abbreviate in some consistant fashion and stick to your own rules. I can probably figure out the rules you're using. You might even mention them in a comment.

Use words with the correct grammatical connotations: nouns for variables, verbs for subroutines, adjectives for . . . Do *not* use clever words (GO TO HELL). Their cuteness wears off very fast and their mnemonic value is too subjective. Besides they offer an unwanted insight into your personality.

Use comments sparingly! (I bet that's welcome.) Remember that program you looked through - the one with all the comments? How helpful were all those comments? How soon did you quit reading them? Programs are self-documenting, even assembler programs, with a modicum of help from mnemonics. It does no good to say:

LA B . Load A with B

In fact, it does positive bad: if I see comments like that I'll quit reading them - and miss the helpful ones.

What comments should say is *what* the program is doing. I have to figure out *how* it's doing it from the instructions anyway. A comment like this is welcome:

COMMENT SEARCH FOR DAMAGED SHIPMENTS

Mnemonics apply to variables and labels (You can even get mnemonic value in FORTRAN statement numbers). Where possible you should apply them to registers also. You may do well to assign several names to the same entity, to indicate its current use. However, don't waste effort naming things that don't need names. If you need a counter, use I, J, K; to assign a big name (EXC-CNTR) to an insignificant variable is no help.

2.5 Routines and subroutines

There are two words I need to establish precise definitions for: A *subroutine* is a set of instructions that return from whence they came. A *routine* is a set of instructions that return to some standard place.

To put it another way, you *jump* to a routine, you *call* a subroutine. The difference is retained in higher-level languages: GO TO versus CALL or ENTER.

So what? Subroutines suffer from nesting. If you call a subroutine from within a subroutine you must somehow save the original return address. I'm sure you can rattle-off a dozen hardware/software ways of doing this. They're all expensive.

If you jump somewhere, not intending to come back, you can save trouble, time and space. But only if you really never come back. To simulate a subroutine call is worse than ever.

Higher-level languages conceal this by nesting automatically. The best solution is to nest if you must, but only when you must, and never to save the same address more than once. That is, upon entering a subroutine, save the return address if you intend to call other subroutines. When you're finally ready to return, then un-nest.

Obvious? Perhaps. But it's usually done wrong! Sometimes the problem only arises with recursive subroutine calls; depending on hardware. It always arises with re-entrant programming.

So we can get in and out of routines and subroutines. How do we pass parameters? Again, there are as many answers as computers, languages and programmers. We shall standardize: you pass what you can in registers; the rest via a push-down stack.

It is extremely important for routines to be able to communicate *efficiently*. I hope you are aware of the cost of a FORTRAN subroutine call. I consider it a basic flaw in the language. We will be moving among so many subroutines that failing to minimize overhead could easily halve our running speed.

You must also consider the value of a subroutine. It isolates a logical function and it eliminates repeated instructions. The first is acceptable only at minimal cost. The second only if space is saved: a 1-instruction subroutine is ridiculous; a 2-instruction must be called from 3 places to break even. Be careful!

Finally, it is important to use registers efficiently. Assign registers for specific purposes and use them consistently. Re-assign registers if you must to avoid conflicts. Do not move data from one register to another; see that it is where it belongs in the first place.

When I say register, I'm obviously thinking assembler. However, you will have to simulate the function of registers with subscripts, etc. in other languages, and the same considerations apply.

3. Programs with input

A program without input is a program with a single task. A program with input may have many tasks, which it will perform as directed by its input. Thus I consider input to be control information, and the control information to define a control language.

We shall have a problem in this chapter, for we are discussing a loop. Each element of the loop depends on its predecessor and successor, and we have nowhere to start. I have done the best I could, but am obliged to refer to things before I define them. Especially in the next section where I try to justify some of the details we'll encounter immediately after.

This chapter is full of details, more than I anticipated when I started it. Although I'm surprised there's so much to say, I think it's all of value. I only caution you not to get lost in the details; the structure, the concept of the program are what is important.

To set the stage, let me briefly outline how our program must operate. You are sitting at a keyboard typing input. You type a string of characters that the computer breaks into words. It finds each word in a dictionary, and executes the code indicated by the dictionary entry, perhaps using parameters also supplied by the entry. The process of reading words, identifying them and executing code for them is certainly not unusual. I am simply trying to systematize the process, to extract the inevitable functions and see that they are efficiently performed.

3.1 Nouns and verbs

I've mentioned the dictionary and we'll soon examine the details required to implement it. But first I'd like to talk a bit about individual entries to try and give you a feel for what we're doing.

We're going to read words from your input, find them in the dictionary, and execute their code. A particular kind of word is a literal, a word that identifies itself:

1 17 -3 .5

We won't find such words in the dictionary, but we can identify them by their appearance. Such words act as if they were in the dictionary, and the code executed for them places them on a push-down stack.

Other words act upon arguments found on this stack, for example:

+ add the last 2 numbers placed on the stack, leave the sum there.

, type the number on top of the stack, and remove it from the stack.

If we type a phrase such as:

1 17 + ,

We are saying: put 1 onto the stack, 17 onto the stack, add them, and type their sum. Each word performs its specific, limited function; independently of any other word. Yet the combination of words achieves something useful. In fact, if we type:

```
4837 758 + -338 + 23 + 4457 + -8354 + ,
```

we can even do something non-trivial: each number is added to the sum of its predecessors, and the result typed.

This is basically the value of our program. It lets us combine simple operations in a flexible way to accomplish a task.

Let's look more closely at the words we used above. They fall into 2 distinct classes; English even provides names for them:

Nouns place arguments onto the stack.

Verbs operate upon arguments on the stack.

All words cause code to be executed. However, in the case of nouns, the code does very little: simply place a number on the stack. Verbs are considerably more varied in their effects. They may do as little as add 2 arguments, or as much as type out a result - which requires a great deal of code.

In effect, nouns place arguments onto the stack in anticipation of verbs that will act upon them. The word anticipation is a good one. In order to keep our verbs simple, we promise that their arguments are available. We could define a verb that reads the next word and uses it as an argument; but in general, we don't. It is not the business of a verb to provide its own arguments; we use nouns to provide arguments before we execute the verb. In fact, this substantially simplifies our program.

We can extend the characterization of entries a little further. Verbs have different numbers of arguments:

Unary verbs modify the number on the stack.

Binary verbs combine 2 arguments to leave a single result.

Arithmetic operations are binary, arithmetic functions are usually unary. However, there are more verbs than we can usefully catagorize. For example, the verb "," that types the stack is not unary, since it removes the number from the stack. Although it does have a single argument.

Another way of distinguishing verbs is:

Destructive verb removes its arguments from the stack.

Non-destructive verb leaves its arguments on the stack.

Unary and binary verbs, as well as the type verb ",", are destructive. The verb DUP, which I define to duplicate the top of the stack, is non-destructive. In general verbs are destructive. In fact, I deliberately define verbs to be destructive in order to simplify the task of remembering which are and which aren't. I recommend that you do the same.

Literals are nouns. We can define other words as nouns; words that use their parameter field to place numbers onto the stack:

Constants place the contents of their parameter field onto the stack.

Variables place the address of their parameter field onto the stack.

For example, if PI is a constant, it places 3.14 onto the stack. Thus:

`1. `PI 2. * / ,

reads: place 1. onto the stack, place 3.14 onto the stack, place 2. onto the stack, multiply (2. and PI), divide (1. by 2PI), and type. Constants are particularly useful when you're using code numbers. It lets you give names to numbers that might otherwise be hard to remember.

However, the most important nouns by far are literals and variables. A variable gives a name to a location and not to a value, as elementary programming texts laboriously explain. However, what higher-level languages conceal is that variables may be used in 2 distinct ways:

To name a location from which a value is to be taken.

To name a location into which a value is to be stored.

A constant automatically performs the first; and inherently prevents the second (you can't store a value into a constant, for you don't know where the constant came from). Rather than try to distinguish function by context, as compilers do, we shall define 2 verbs that act upon variables:

@ replace the address on the stack with its contents.

= Store into the address on the stack, the value just beneath it on the stack.

Thus if I type, where X is a variable,

`X @ ,`

I mean: place the address of X onto the stack, fetch its value, and type. And if I type,

`X @ Y @ + ,`

I mean: fetch the value of X, the value of Y, add, and type. On the other hand,

`X @ Y =`

will: fetch the address of X, then its value, fetch the address of Y, and store the value of X into Y. But if I type

`X Y =`

I'm saying: fetch the address of X, the address of Y, and store the address of X into Y. Maybe this is that I mean to do, it's not unreasonable.

I don't want to belabor the point, for we're getting ahead of ourselves. But variables require special verbs, one of which (@) is not ordinarily explicit. Incidently, I originally used the word VALUE for @. But the verb is used so often it deserves a single character name, and I thought @ (at) had some mnemonic value, besides being otherwise useless.

I urge you to adopt the vereb @. Although you can conceal it in various ways - we'll discuss one later - it adds needless complication. Such a useful verb oughtn't be invisible. Besides it lets you store addresses in variables - indirect addressing

```
X Y = Y @ @ ,
```

reads: store the address of X in Y; place the address of Y on the stack, fetch its value (the address of X) fetch *its* value (the contents of X), and type.

I hope I've given you some idea of how you can put arguments onto the stack and act on them with verbs. Although I define constants and variables, unary and binary verbs, I hope it's clear that these are only examples. You must define the nouns and verbs and perhaps other kinds of words that are useful for your application.

In fact, I think that is what programming is all about. If you have available a program such as I will now describe, once you decide what entries an application requires, you'll find it absolutely trivial to code those entries, and thus complete your problem.

3.2 Control loop

Our program has a structure that is easy to miss: it is a single loop. However, it is a loop that is diffuse - scattered among all the code in the program. Very few instructions are gathered together to form an identifiable loop, so the loop warrants some explanation.

We are going to read a word from the input string, look up that word in the dictionary, and jump to the routine it specifies. Each routine will return to the top of the loop to read another word. We will be discussing many routines and it will be helpful to have a term to identify "return to the top of the loop to read another word". I will use the word RETURN; you should provide a standard macro or label in your program for the same purpose.

Actually, you accomplish 2 purposes: you mark the end of a routine. And you identify the preceeding code as being a routine, as distinct from a subroutine. Thus, I use the word RETURN with a totally different meaning from the FORTRAN RETURN statement. I shall speak of EXITing from a subroutine.

Included in your control loop should be a check that the parameter stack has not exceeded its limits. This is best done after RETURNing from a routine, and only needs to be done for routines that use the stack. Thus, there are 2 possible RETURN points (actually 3).

The control loop must be efficient. If you count the instructions it contains, you measure the overhead associated with your program. You will be executing some very small routines, and it's embarrassing to find overhead dominating machine use. In particular you don't need to check other than the parameter stack.

One more routine belongs in this section: an error routine. Whenever an error is detected, a routine should jump to ERROR which will type the offending word and an error message. It will then reset all stacks and the input pointer and RETURN normally.

The problem of how to treat error messages is an important one. We are in a position to do a good job: to avoid setting and testing flags; to avoid cascading back through subroutine calls. By clearing the return stack, we eliminate any pending subroutine returns. By not returning with an error flag, we avoid having the subroutine have to worry about errors. This simplifies the code, but we must have a standard method of handling problems.

The image of a person at a keyboard in invaluable for this purpose. No matter what problem arises, we needn't worry about what to do. Pass the buck; ask the user. For example, he types a word not in the dictionary. What to do? Ask him: type the word and an error message, in this case "?". He tries to add 2 numbers and there's only 1 on the stack: type the word and "STACK!". He tries to access a field beyond the limit of his memory: type the word and "LIMIT!".

Of course, you want to be careful not to pose the user problems he can't solve. Faced with a message "MEMORY PARITY" what can he do about it? But he's certainly in a better position than your program to take corrective action to most problems. And of course it's up to you to decide what situations are problems.

By the way. Since you don't check the stack until after you executed a routine, it will exceed stack limits before you know it. Thus, stack overflow and underflow should be non-fatal. A good solution is to let the parameter stack overflow into the return stack, and underflow into the message buffer. The return stack should never underflow.

3.3 Word subroutine

I've described the control loop that will run our program. The first thing it does is to read a word; so, the first thing we shall discuss is how to read a word.

What is a word? Not a computer word, as I'm sure you realise, although we shall have to use the word "word" in that sense. A word is a string of characters bounded by spaces. It is extracted from a larger string of characters by the routine we are discussing.

Let me contrast this definition with more conventional input routines. FORTRAN formatted input, for example, doesn't speak of words but of fields. The meaning of a number is determined by the field it resides in; that is, by its position on a card. Since we are not using cards, the notion of position becomes clumsy and we replace it with order: The order of the words we read is significant, though their position is not. We lose, however, the ability to leave a field empty, since we cannot recognise an empty word. All our data must be explicit, which is probably a good idea but a slow one to learn. Decide now that you will not specify input conventions that have optional parameters.

Very well, let's write the WORD subroutine. It uses the input pointer to point at the current position in the source text, the output pointer to point at the current position in memory where we will move the word. We must move it; partly to align it on a computer-word boundary and partly because we may want to modify it.

Fetch input characters and discard them so long as they're spaces. Thereafter deposit them until you find another space. Deposit this space and as many others as needed to fill out the last computer-word. If you have a character-oriented machine you may be amused at my insistence on word-alignment. Mainly I'm anticipating the search subroutine when we'll want to compare as large a piece of the word as possible. If a word holds 6 characters (or even 2) it's much more efficient to compare them in parallel than serially, even if you have the hardware.

You may want to set an upper limit on word length. Such a limit should include the largest number you will be using. Then the question arises as to what to do with a longer word. You might simply discard the excess characters, providing you don't plan to dissect the word (Chapter 8). Better, perhaps, that you force a space into the word at the limit. That is, break the word into 2 words. Presumably something's wrong and you will eventually discover it in attempting to process the fragments. However, this limit should be large enough - 10 to 20 characters - so that it does not constitute a real restriction on your input. It should also be 1 character less than a multiple of your computer-word length, so that you can always include the terminal space in the aligned word.

Words are bounded by spaces. You can probably find objections to such a simple definition. For instance, arithmetic expressions often do not have spaces between words. We shall discuss this in Chapter 9. Let me just say that we need to embed periods, dashes, and other characters in words in order not to unreasonably restrict our potential vocabulary. We'd like these to be words:

```
1,000   1.E-6   I.B.M.   B&O   4'3"   $4.95
```

3.3.1 Message I/O

The WORD subroutine presumably examines input characters. Where does it get these characters?

Although it's possible to read cards, I'm going to assume that you have a keyboard to type input. Now there are 2 kinds of keyboards, buffered and unbuffered. A buffered keyboard stores the message until you type an end-of-message character. An unbuffered keyboard sends each character as you type it. Your hardware, in turn, may buffer input for you or not.

In any case we may want to examine each character more than once, so we want buffered input. Even if you can process characters as they arrive, don't. Store them into a message buffer.

Set aside a 1-line message buffer. Its size is the maximum size of a message, either input or output, so if you plan to use a 132 positions printer make it large enough.

If you simulate buffering, you should implement a backspace character and a cancel message character. For you will make a lot of typing errors. If your hardware buffers, but does not provide these capabilities, you should do so. This probably means a prescan of the input; any other technique gets too complicated, and probably costs more in the end.

Mark the end of an input message with an end-of-message word. This is a word bounded by spaces like any other. It may or may not coincide with the end-of-message character that you typed, depending on your hardware and character set as to whether the required spaces can be provided. This word permits ready detection of the last word in a message. It will have a specific definition and perform a valuable task.

In addition to a keyboard, you must have some sort of output device: a printer or scope. Again, it may be buffered or unbuffered. Unlike input, we have no reason not to use unbuffered output. However, if you have several output devices, odds are one is buffered. If so, treat them all as buffered, simulating the buffering where needed.
We will use the same message buffer for both input and output. My motivation is to save space, or rather to increase the utilization of space. My reasoning is that input and output are mutually exclusive. There are exceptions, but we don't usually read input and prepare output simultaneously. At least we never have to.

However, we do need a switch (1 bit) that states whether the message buffer still contains input. The first time (or perhaps everytime) we type output, we must reset this switch. We'll use it later.

We need a receive subroutine that will exit when we have a complete input message. Likewise, a transmit subroutine that will exit after sending an output message. It should await an acknowledgement if the hardware provides one. Don't try to overlap transmission of one message with preparation of the next. Transmission is so slow and preparation so fast that no noticable increase in speed is available. And it complicates the program considerably.

3.3.2 Moving characters

I will speak of fetching and depositing characters several times, mostly concerned with input and output. For example, the WORD subroutine moves characters from the message buffer to a word buffer. A simple task conceptually, but a difficult one to implement. We would have exactly the same problem moving arrays from place to place. But in fact, we needn't move arrays and we must move characters.

Let us define 2 entities: an input pointer and an output pointer. For the moment you can think of them as index registers, although we will have to generalize later. Let's also write 2 subroutines, although your hardware may permit them to be instructions: FETCH will load the character identified by the input pointer into a register and advance the input pointer; DEPOSIT will store that register at the position identified by the output pointer and advance the output pointer.

Depending on your computer, FETCH and DEPOSIT can be veery simple, or extremely complex. If they require more than 1 instruction, they should be subroutines, for we'll use them often. By combining them, we can perform a move. However, it's important to be able to examine the character before depositing it. A hardware move instruction is of little value.

The input and output pointers use index registers. However, those registers should only be used during a move. They should be loaded prior to a move and saved after it, for they will be used for a number of purposes, and it becomes impractical to store anything there permanently.

3.4 Decimal conversion

After isolating and aligning a word from the input string, your control loop searches the dictionary for it. If it isn't in the dictionary, it might be a number. A number is a special kind of word that doesn't need a dictionary entry; by examining the word itself we can decide what to do with it. The code executed for a number will place the binary representation of the number onto the stack.

We will discuss the stack in the next section. First let's define a number more precisely.

3.4.1 Numbers

It is very hard to state exactly what is a number and what is not. You will have to write a NUMBER subroutine to convert numbers to binary, and this subroutine is the definition of a number. If it can convert a word to binary, that word is a number; otherwise not.

It is foolish to examine a word to see if it is a number, and then to convert the number to binary. Examination and conversion can be combined into one process very easily.

There is one kind of word that invariably is a number: a string of digits possible prefixed with a minus. Such numbers are usually converted to binary integers. For example:

`1 4096 -3 7777 0 00100 10000000 6AF2 -B`

are some decimal, octal and hex numbers. The number does not specify its base, and a word that may be a hexadecimal number, may not be a decimal number.

So already base has complicated numbers. And beyond simple integers are endless other kinds of numbers: fixed-point fractions, floating-point fractions double-precision integers, complex fractions, etc. And such numbers can have many different formats as words: decimal point, implied decimal point, exponents, and suffixes. Indeed, the same word may represent different numbers depending on its context.

One of your major tasks will be to decide what kinds of numbers you need for your application, how you will format them, and how you will convert them. Each kind of number must be uniquely identifiable by the NUMBER subroutine, and for each you must provide an output conversion routine.

I suggest the following guidelines: always define integers and negative integers; do not permit a prefixed plus sign, it is useless on a number and useful as a word; if you have floating-point hardware, distinguish floating-point fractions by a decimal point; if you lack floating-point hardware, use the decimal point to identify fixed-point fractions; don't simulate floating-point; don't permit exponents on fractions. These rules permit a simple NUMBER subroutine which I will outline.

Your application may need special number formats:

45'6 for 45 ft. 6 in., an integer

1,000,000   an integer

$45.69   an integer

It is not hard to include such numbers in NUMBER, but you cannot include all possible formats. Some are incompatible:

3'9 for 3 ft. 9 in.

12'30 for 12 min. 30 sec. of arc

12'30 for 12 min. 30 sec. of time

4'6 for 4 shillings 6 pence

Basic Principle!

Fixed-point numbers are rarely used. I am convinced of their value and would like to show you. With floating-point hardware, they offer only the advantage of greater significance, which is probably not worth much. However, without floating-point hardware they offer most of the capabilities of floating-point numbers, without the very great cost of floating-point software. The exception is a wide range of exponents.

I am convinced that exponents are badly misused on computers. Most applications use real numbers that can be used on a desk-calculator - say between 10^6 and 10^{-6}. Such numbers can be equally well represented in fixed-point format. Floating-point is not needed, although if hardware is available it might as well be used. There are cases, especially in physics, when large exponents occur - 10^{43} or 10^{-13}. But this usually indicates that the proper units have not been chosen, or maybe even that logarithms should be used.

Of course, compilers do not implement fixed-point, so people don't use it. We are in a position to implement it, and to take advantage of the speed possible with fixed-point (integer) instructions. What does a fixed-point number look like? Choose the number of decimal places you want to use. You may change this from time-to-time, but shouldn't mix numbers with different precision. Have your NUMBER subroutine align all numbers (with decimal points) as if you had typed exactly that number of decimal places. Thereafter treat that number like an integer. That is, if you choose 3 decimal places:

1. is considered 1.000 and treated as 1000

3.14 is 3.140 and 3140

2.71828 is 2.718 and 2718

-.5 is -.500 and -500

I wouldn't bother rounding unless your application demanded it, or your hardware made it easy.

You can add and subtract such numbers without concern; their decimal points are aligned. After multiplying 2 numbers, you must divide by 1000 to re-align the decimal points. Hardware usually facilitates this; the result of a multiply is a double-precision product in the proper position for a dividend. Before dividing 2 numbers, you must multiply the dividend by 1000 to maintain precision and align the decimal points. Again, this is easy.

So, providing your words are large enough to store the number of decimal places you need, fixed-point arithmetic is easy. If you have the hardware, double-precision numbers and operations let you deal with larger numbers. Just as easily. And much easier than simulating floating-point operations. You may have to write your own square-root and trig-function subroutines, but there are approximations available that make this not-difficult. And they'll be much faster than the equivalent simulated floating-point subroutines.

Aligning decimal points is easy to visualize and avoids truncation problems. However, you may prefer to align binary points. That is, instead of 3 decimal places, keep 10 binary places to the right of the point. The multiplication and division by 1000 can then be replaced by binary shifts - the equivalent for binary - which are much faster.

You must balance the gain in speed against the problem of alignment during conversion (input and output) and truncation during multiplication and division being more subtle. And possibly the difficulty of explaining your arithmetic.

3.4.2 Input conversion

Now let's discuss the NUMBER subroutine in detail. First, why is it a subroutine? If you examine the program I've outlined so far, and even the program as augmented by the end of the book, you'll fiind NUMBER is called only once - in the control loop. By my own rules NUMBER should thus be in-line code. However, I can't bring myself to put it in line; the logic in NuMBER is so complex that I want to isolate it away from the control loop, to emphasize its logical function - one purpose of a subroutine - and to reduce confusion in the control loop itself; also, I'm never confident that I won't want to call NUMBER from some other routine, in fact I have. But I think that such violations of programming standards should be explicitly recognised.

The key to a good NUMBER subroutine is another subroutine that it calls. This subroutine has 2 entry points: SIGNED tests the next character for minus, sets a switch, zeros number-so-far and falls into NATURAL. NATURAL fetches characters, tests that they're digits, multiplies the number-so-far by 10 and adds the digit. It repeats until it finds a non-digit.

With this routine, NUMBER can work as follows: set the input pointer to the start of the aligned word, call SIGNED. If the stopping character is a decimal point, clear counter, call NATURAL to get the fraction, and use counter to choose a power-of-ten to convert to a floating or fixed-point fraction. In any case, apply SIGNED's switch to make number-so-far negative. Exit.

The routine that calls NUMBER can test the stopping character:

If it is a space, the conversion was successful.

Otherwise, the word was not a number.

For example, the following are numbers:

0 3.14 -17 -.5

The following are not:

0- 3.14. +17 -.5Z X 6.-3 1.E3

In each case NUMBER will stop on a non-space. The number-so-far will be correctly converted up to that point (possibly 0) but it is of no value.

SIGNED/NATURAL is a valid subroutine since it is called twice. Moreover, if you define other number formats, you'll find it useful. For example, the format ft'in

After calling SIGNED, if the stopping character is a ' multiply number-so-far by 12 and call NATURAL. Then proceed as usual, testing for decimal point.

If you want to verify that "in" are less than 12, you'll want to modify this slightly.

In NATURAL the number-so-far is multipled by 10. Don't use a litereal 10, but rather define a field (BASE) and store a 10 there as multiplier. Then you can change BASE to 8 (or 16) and handle octal numbers. You can even change it to 2 to use binary numberes. NATURAL should test for digits by comparing them with BASE, thus prohibiting 9 in an octal number. Hexadecimal input numbers cause an additional problem because the digits A-Z do not follow 9 in standard character sets. It is thus harder to recognise digits; but this problem is isolated in a single place (NATURAL) and is easy to code:

An origin must usually be subtracted from a digit to get its binary value. If BASE is 16, a different origin is subtracted from A-F.

NUMBER should be efficient, at least in recognising words that are not numbers. Not so much because you will use so many numbers, but because you will examine many words that aren't numbers. We will discuss this further in Chapter 8. It is also important that you examine the aligned copy of a word. There are several reasons: to avoid trouble with the input pointer, to guarantee a terminal space.

However, this creates a problem: the largest number you will use must fit in the aligned word; this may require a longer word than you would otherwise use. A number longer than word-size will have its right-most digits discarded. This will probably not destroy its numeric appearance so that no error will be detected; but the conversion will be incorrect. This problem is not serious, just be aware of it.

3.4.3 Output conversion

Numeric output is harder than numeric input because there is an extra step involved. During input, you multiply the number by 10 and add each digit. You can work from left to right. During output, you divide by 10, save the remainder for the digit, and repeat with the quotient until it becomes 0. You get the digits from right to left, but you want to type them from left to right.

Thus, you need somewhere to store the digits temporarily. A good place is the far end of the message buffer. The space is unused since you presumably have enough space for the number. Of course, you can use the stack. If you place a space at the right end of your temporary storage, and then deposit the digits from right to left, you can use the TYPE$_B$ subroutine to finally type the number.

You'll probably want to handle both negative numbers and fractions. Remember the number is negative and work with its absolute value. After you're finished, prefix a minus. Fractions require 2 conversion loops: one to convert the fraction, counting the number of digits and depositing a decimal point; another to convert the integer, stopping when the quotient becomes 0. You don't want to test the quotient in the fraction.

If you take the care, and spend a couple of instructions, you can improve the appearance of your numbers by:

Not typing a decimal point if the number has no decimal places.

Not typing a leading zero to the left of the decimal point.

You will probably have several dictionary entries specifying different output formats. For example, each kind of number: integer, float, complex will need its own output routine. However, the actual conversion should be done by a single subroutine with parameters to distinguish special cases. That is, a single subroutine inverse to the NUMBER subroutine. The similarities among different numbers are much greater than their differences.

If you use decimal fixed-point fractions, you already have a field D that specifies the number of decimal places. The same field is used to control decimal placement on output. Ordinarily decimal places on input and output will be the same. Even with floating-point numbers you need that field, since you're rarely interested in full precision output.

If you want to produce reports - carefully formatted columns of numbers - you will need to right-justify numbers. That is, to line up decimal points. For this you need another parameter F, the width of the field in which the number is to be right-justified. It's easy to use: after converting the number right-left, compute the number of spaces you need and call SPACE. Then call $TYPE_B$. In determining spaces, remember that $TYPE_B$ always types a space *after* the number. Thus, you will always have at least a single space between numbers. If the number won't fit in the field you specify, you'll still have that one space, and the full number will be typed - fouling up the report format - but showing you the bad number.

Let me acknowledge that if you are going to right-justify numbers you can place the digits directly into position from right to left, for you know where the rightmost digit must go. But then you must space-fill the message buffeer before starting output, and you can't type unbuffered output immediately. However, my main objection is that you can't compose free-format output. For example, place a number in a sentence without extra leading spaces. And very often unformatted output is adequate, saving you having to specify field sizes you don't care about.

Depending on your formatting requirements, there are other dictionary entries you might want: A SPACE entry, to space the number of positions on the stack. It can even space backwards - by changing the output pointer - if the stack is negative. This is useful if you want to suppress that space provided by TYPE$_B$. A tab entry might calculate the amount to space in order to reach a specific position on the stack.

3.5 Stacks

We will be using several push-down stacks and I want to make sure you can implement them. A push-down stack operates in a last-in first-out fashion. It is composed of an array and a pointer. The pointer identifies the last word placed in the array. To place a word onto the stack you must advance the pointer and store the word (in that order). To take a word off the stack you must fetch the word and drop the pointer (in that order). There is no actual pushing-down involved, though the effect is the same.

A stack pointer is an excellent use for an index register, if you have enough. Indirect addressing is also a possibility, especially if you have an add-to-memory instruction.

3.5.1 Return stack

This stack stores return information. One use is to store the return address for subroutines, when subroutine calls use an index register. The last-in first-out nature of a stack is exactly the behavior required for nested subroutine calls. We will later encounter several other kinds of return information that can be stored in the same stack. It is important not to attempt to combine the return stack and the parameter stack. They are not synchronized. 8 words is probably enough space for the return stack.

3.5.2 Parameter stack

This stack is the one I intend when I say simply stack. Numbers, constants, variables are all placed on this stack, as will be discussed later. This stack is used to pass parameters among routines. Each routine can find its arguments there, regardless of how many other parameters are present, or how long ago they were placed there. You should not implement a parameter stack less than 16 words long.

A valuable refinement to the parameter stack is to set aside a register to hold the word on top of the stack. Several rules must be religiously observed if this is not to cause trouble:

You must never use this register for any other purpose.

You must keep this register full; no flag to indicate that it's empty.

If you cannot fulfill these conditions, you're better off with the stack entirely in core.

We need some terminology:

You *place* a word *onto* then stack, thereby increasing its size.

You *drop* a word *from* the stack, thereby decreasing its size.

The word on top of the stack is called the *top* word.

The word immediately below the top of the stack is called the *lower* word.

You may need to control the parameter stack from the input. These words (dictionary entries) are extremely useful, and illustrate the terminology above:

DROP drop the top word from the stack.

DUP place the top word onto the stack, thereby duplicating it.

SWAP exchange the top and lower words.

OVER place the lower word onto the stack; move it over the top word.

3.6 Dictionary

Every program with input must have a dictionary. Many programs without input have dictionaries. However, these are often not recognised as such. A common 'casual' dictionary is a series of IF . . . ELSE IF . . . ELSE IF . . . statements, or their equivalent. Indeed, this is a reasonable implementation if the dictionary is small (8 entries) and non-expandable.

It is important to acknowledge the function and existence of a dictionary, to concentrate it in a single place and to standardize the format of entries. A common characteristic of bad programs is that the equivalent of a dictionary is scattered all over the program at great cost in space, time and apparant complexity.

The most important property of an entry is one that is usually overlooked. Each entry should identify a routine that is to be executed. Very often many entries execute the same routine. Perhaps there are few routines to choose among. This tends to conceal the importance of specifying what is to be done for each entry. By placing the address of a routine in each entry, an optimal and standard procedure for getting to that code can be designed.

Significantly, the IF . . . ELSE IF construction has the characteristic of associating a routine with each entry.

3.6.1 Entry format

There are 2 distinct ways to organize dictionary entries. The choice may depend upon hardware characteristics, but I recommend the second. A dominant feature of entries is that they have variable length. A part of the entry may be the code to be executed, or parameters or an area of storage, all of which may have arbitrary length.

One possibility is to split an entry into two portions, one of fixed size, one of variable size. This permits scanning fixed size entries to identify a word and often there are hardware instructions to speed this search. A part of the fixed entry can be a link to a variable area; of course, you choose the fixed size so as to make the link in the nature of an overflow - an exception.

However, since input is relatively small volume (even as augmented in definitions), to minimize the time required to search the dictionary does not lead to a global optimum. You can gain greater flexibility, a simpler allocation of core, and ultimately greater speed by chaining the variable-sized entries together directly. This is the organization I shall discuss.

An entry has 4 fields: the word being defined, the code to be executed, a link to the next entry and parameters. Each of these warrants discussion.

The format of a word must be decided in conjunction with the word input routine. It should have a fixed size which may be smaller than that defined by NEXT, but must be a multiple of hardware word size. However, more sophisticated applications use the dictionary words to construct output messages. Then it is important not to truncate words, in which case the word field must have variable length. To mark the size of this field the terminal space should be used rather than a character count. To handle a variable word field within a variable entry, the word should extend in one direction (backwards) and the parameter in the other (forwards). Fixed or variable word size requires application of the Basic Principle.

The code field should contain the address of a routine rather than an index to a table or other abbreviation. Program efficiency depends strongly on how long it takes to get to the code once a entry is identified, as discussed in 3.9. However, the small size of your program may permit this address to fit in less space than the hardware address field.

The link field may likewise be smaller than hardware-specified. It should contain the absolute location of the next entry rather than its distance from the current entry.

The parameter field will typically contain 4 kinds of information:

A number, constant or variable, of variable size. The nature of the number is determined by the code it executes.

Space in which numbers will be stored - an array. The size of the array may be a parameter or may be implicit in the code executed.

A definition: an array of dictionary entries representing virtual-computer instructions; see 3.9.

Machine instructions: code compiled by your program which is itself executed for this entry. Such data must probably be aligned on word boundary, the other need not.

3.6.2 Search strategies

One basic principle applies to dictionary search: it must be backwards - from latest to oldest entries. You have perhaps noticed that the dictionary is *not* arranged in any order (ie. alphabetical) other than that in which entries are made. This permits the same word to be re-defined, and the latest meaning to be obtained. There is no trade-off valuable enough to compromise this property.

To identify a word, place it (or its first portion) in a register and compare for equality with each entry (or its first portion). An algebraic comparison is adequate. Concern is sometimes expressed that treating words as floating-point numbers may permit a false equality. This has 0 probablity and you can always change the word - ignore it.

A full-word compare (rather than a character-by-character) should be used for speed. A match is usually found on the first portion, and extensions may be treated with less efficiency (though still full-word compares).

Fixed-length entries may be scanned with a simple loop. Linked entries require an equally simple loop, but usually a slower one. However, the speed of a linked search can be increased without limit: Rather than link each entry to its physical predecessor, link it to a predecessor in one of a number of chains. Scramble the word to determine which chain it belongs in, both when you enter it and when you search for it. Thus, only a fraction of the total dictionary need be searched to find the word or assure its absence.

The number of chains should be a power of 2: 8 will provide a useful increase in speed. The scramble technique may be very simple: add the first few characters together and use the low-order bits. In order to maintain a linked dictionary, the next available location and the location of the last entry must be kept. A multiply-chained dictionary requires the location of the last entry for each chain: a small price in space for a large gain in time.

However, search time is not a important consideration, and I advise against multiple chains unless the dictionary is very large (hundreds of entries).

3.6.3 Initialization

The dictionary is built into your program and is presumably initialized by your compiler. This is centainly true if you have fixed-size entries. Variable-sized entries must be linked together, however, and this can be beyond the ability of your compiler, especially if you have multiple chains.

In such a case, it is a simple matter to write a loop that scans the dictionary and establishes the links. It should scan the core occupied by the dictionary and recognise an entry by some unique flag (7's in the link field). It can the pick up the word, scramble it and add it to the appropriate chain.

This is purely temporary code. Although it may call permanent subroutines to scramble and link, the initialization code will have no further use. Thus, it should be placed where it can be overlaid as the program proceeds. The message buffer, if large enough, or the disk buffer are possibilities.

Other things may need initializing, particularly any registers that are assigned specific tasks. All such duties should be concentrated in this one place.

3.7 Control language – an example

Applications tend to be complicated before they become interesting. But here's a fairly common problem that shows off a control language to advantage. Implementation would be tricky, execution woud be inefficient; but the program would be simple, and its application flexible.

The problem is to examine a sequential file, select certain records, sort them, and list them - in many different ways. Suppose these variables define the fields in the record:

NAME AGE SALARY DEPT JOB SENIORITY

Let's define these verbs:

LIST SORT EQUAL GREATER LESS

Each acts upon the temporary file produced by the previous, in accordance with the following examples:

List in alphabetical order all employees in dept 6:

```
6 DEPT EQUAL NAME SORT LIST
```

First we choose records with dept = 6 and copy them into a temporary file. Then we sort that file by name. Then we list it.

List twice, by seniority, all employees holding job 17 in dept 3:

```
17 JOB EQUAL 3 DEPT EQUAL SENIORITY SORT LIST LIST
```

List, by age, all employees whose salary is greater than $10,000; and identify those whose seniority is less than 3:

10000 SALARY GREATER AGE SORT LIST 3 SENIORITY LESS LIST

Several comments seem indicated. We can apply a logical "and" by using several select verbs in sequence; we cannot use a logical "or". We can sort on several fields, if our sorting technique does not unnecessarily re-arrange records. We need 2 more verbs:

REWIND END

to start over with the original file, and to quit.

Actually, many other capabilities could be provided, including the ability to locate specific records and modify them. But rather than design a particular application, I just want to show how nouns and verbs combine to provide great flexibility with a simple program. Notice how even such a simple example uses all our facilities: the word subroutine, the number subroutine, the dictionary, the stack. We're not speculating, we are providing essential code.

4. Programs that grow

So far our dictionary has been static. It contains all the entries you need - placed there when the program was compiled. This need not be. We can define entries that will cause additional entries to be made and deleted. Let me point out why this might be desirable.

You have a program that controls an application. Based upon the words you type, it will do as you direct. In Chapter 3 we provided the ability to type out results. Not the sort of results that are the inevitable result of the application, but variables that you'd maybe like to see. More a conversational sort of output, since it is controlled directly by input.

There are 2 problems with this situation. First, to add an entry to your dictionary you must re-compile the program. Clearly, you won't be adding many entries - but maybe you won't have to. Second, all your entries must be present at the same time. This creates, not so much a volume problem, as a complexity problem. If your application is complex, it becomes increasingly difficult to make all aspects compatible. For instance, to find distinct names for all fields. Third, if you find an error in an entry you must recompile the program. You have no ability to correct an entry - though of course you could define entries to provide that ability.

If you can create dictionary entries you can accomplish 2 things: You can apply your program to different aspects of your application - without conflicts and reducing complexity. You can create a dictionary entry differently, and thus correct an error. In fact, the purpose of your program undergoes a gradual but important change. You started with a program that controlled an application. You now have a program that provides the capability to control an application. In effect, you have moved up a level from language to meta-language. This is an extremely important step. It may not be productive. It leads you from talking *to* your application to talking *about* your application.

Another way of viewing the transition is the entries in your dictionary. At first they were words that executed pieces of code that constituted your application program. A purely control function. Now they tend to become words that let you construct your application program. They conststitute a problem-oriented-language. The distinction need not be abrupt, but it is irreversible. You change from an application to a system programmer - your system being your application.

I hesitate to say whether this is good or bad. By now you surely know - it depends on the application. I suspect any application of sufficient complexity, and surely any application of any generality, must develop a specialized language. Not a control language, but a descriptive language.

Some examples: A simulator does not want a control language. It is important to be able to describe with great facility the system being simulated. A linear-programming problem needs a language that can describe the problem. A compiler actually provides a descriptive language for use with the programs it compiles. A compiler-compiler describes compilers. What is a compile-compiler that can execute the compiler it describes and in turn execute the program it compiled? That is the question!

Let me now assume that you have a problem that qualifies for a descriptive language. What dictionary entries do you need?

4.1 Adding dictionary entries

Let us now assume that you want to expand your dictionary; that you have a sufficiently complex application to justify a specialized language. How do you make a dictionary entry?

Recall the control loop: it reads a word and searches the dictionary. If you want to define a word, you must not let the control loop see it. Instead you must define an entry that will read the next word and use it before RETURNing to the control loop. In effect, it renders the following word invisible. It must call the word subroutine, which is why it is a subroutine rather than a routine. Let us call such an entry a *defining* entry, its purpose is to define the next word.

In principle we only need one defining entry, but we must supply as a parameter the address of the code to be executed for the entry it defines. Remember that 4 fields are required for each entry: the word, its code address, a link, and (optionally) parameters. The word we obtain from the word subroutine; the link we construct; the parameters we take from the stack. We could also take the address from the stack, but it's more convenient to have a separate defining word for each kind of entry to be constructed. That is, to have a separate defining entry for each address we need, that provides the address from its parameter field.

I'm afraid this is confusing. We have one entry that supplies the address field of a new entry from its own parameter field. Let's take an example; suppose we want to define a constant:

0 CONSTANT ZERO

0 is placed on the stack; the code for the word CONSTANT reads the next word, ZERO, and constructs a dictionary entry for it: it establishes the link to a previous entry, stores 0 from the stack into the parameter field, and from its own parameter field stores the address of the code ZERO will execute. This is, presumably, the address of code that will place the contents of the parameter field onto the stack.

Thus, for each kind of entry we will be making, we need a defining entry to supply the code address and do the work. Since all defining entries have much in common, you should write an ENTRY subroutine they can call. It should have as parameter the code address, and construct all of the new entry except the parameter field, which is specialized by the defining entry.

Other defining entries might be:

0 INTEGER I - an integer-size parameter field is initialized to 0; its address will be placed on the stack.

1. REAL X - a floating-point parameter field is initialized to 1.

8 ARRAY TEMP - an 8-word parameter field is cleared to 0; the address of its 1st word will be placed on the stack.

I must emphasize the word "might". Different applications will require different defining entries; even the same word might act differently for different applications. But you are in a position to define any kind of noun you need, and then create as many instances of that noun as you like. It is a futile exercise to attempt to establish a universal set of nouns. Compiler languages have repeatedly stumbled by not providing enough, and no matter how many they provide, someone will want one more.

For example, you might define the following noun:

0 8 INDEX J - J is defined to be an index, that varies from 0 to 8. When executed, it adds its value to the top of the stack.

If you then define appropriate verbs to advance, test and reset J, you can have a powerful indexing facility. Or define:

3 VECTOR X 3 VECTOR Y 9 VECTOR Z

and define arithmetic verbs to implement vector arithmetic:

X Z = Z Y + add X and Y, store in Z.

X Y Z *C multiply X and Y (outer product), store in Z.

Anything you need for your application you can define. But you can never define everything. Basic Principle!

4.2 Deleting entries

So far we've only discussed defining nouns. Actually, you'll be using more verbs than nouns, but they require much longer explanations. Here is one kind of verb.

If you can add entries to your dictionary, eventually you're going to want to get rid of them. You'll need to delete entries in order to re-enter them correctly or delete entries in order to make room for another application. After all, your dictionary is finite; no matter how large you make it, you will be aware of its upper limit. Parkinson's Law may be rephrased: Dictionaries expand to fill the available space.

There is only one feasible way to delete entries. That is to delete all entries after a certain point. If you were to delete specific entries, you would leave holes in the dictionary, since it occupies contiguous core. If you attempt to pack the dictionary to recover the holes, you are faced with a wicked re-location problem, since we use absolute addresses. To avoid absolute addresses is inefficient and unnecessary.

Deleting trailing entries is a completely satisfactory solution. I know of no argument to prove thie, except to say try it and see. You'll find that, in practice, you add a bunch of entries; find a problem; delete those entries; fix the problem; and reenter all the entries. Or you fill your dictionary for one application; clear it; and re-fill with another application. Or you might re-load the same application just to clear some fields. In each case, you want to get rid of all the latest entries.

One exception is when you use some entries to construct others. The constructing entries are then no longer needed, and there is no way to get rid of them. It happens; I may even give some examples later. But all you lose is dictionary space, and I can't see a practical solution.

OK, how do you delete trailing entries? You want to mark a point in your dictionary and reset evereything to that position. One thing is the dictionary pointer that identifies the next available word in the dictionary. That's easy. However, you must reset the chain heads that identify the previous entry for each of your search chains. It only takes a small loop: follow each chain back, as you do when searching, until you find a link that preceeds your indicated point.

If you have fixed-size entries, you must reset the pointer to the parameter area, but you don't have to follow links.

A convenient way to specify the point you want to delete from is to place a special entry there. A verb that will delete itself and evereything following it when you execute it. For example,

REMEMBER HERE

is a defining entry. When you type HERE, it is forgotten; it both marks a place in the dictionary and executes the deleting code. HERE doesn't need a parameter field, unless you use fixed-length entries, whereupon it must save the current value of the parameter pointer. This is our first example of a verb-defining entry.

4.3 Operations

Recall that the stack is where arguments are found. There are some words you may want to define to provide arithmetic capabilities. They are of little value to a control language, but essential to add power to it. I'll use logical constructs TRUE (1) and FALSE (0). And remember the definition of top and lower from 3.6.

Unary operators: change the number on top of the stack.

MINUS changes sign of top.

ABS sets sign positive.

ZERO if top is zero, replace it with TRUE; otherwise place FALSE onto the stack.

NONZERO if top is nonzero, place TRUE onto the stack; otherwise leave it alone (leave FALSE on the stack).

Binary operators: Remove top from the stack and replace lower by a function of both.

+ add top to lower.

* multiply lower by top.

- subtract top from lower.

/ divide lower by top, leave the quotient.

MOD divide lower by top, leave the remainder.

MAX if top is larger than lower, replace lower by top.

MIN if top is smaller than lower, replace lower by top.

** raise lower to power of top.

These are only samples. Clearly you are free to define whatever words you feel useful. Keep in mind that you must place the arguments on the stack before you operate on them. Numbers are automatically placed on the stack. Constants are too. Thus, the following make sense:

1 2 +

PI 2. *

1 2 + 3 * 7 MOD 4 MAX

1 2 3 + *

This notation permits arithmetic calculation in the same manner a desk calculator. It is often called parenthesis-free representation or perhaps right-handed Polish, but it is simply the way you work with arguments on a stack. Conventional algebraic notation is much harder to implement (8.2).

Other binary operations are the arithmetic relations: these leave a truth value on the stack:

= are they equal?

< is top greater than lower?
> is top less than lower?
>= is top not greater than lower?
<= is top not less than lower?

The logical operations include a unary and several binary:

NOT if top is FALSE, replace with TRUE; otherwise replace with FALSE.

OR logical or.

AND logical and.

IMP logical implication.

XOR logical exclusive or.

Your stack must have a fixed word-length. However, the operations mentioned above might apply to several kinds of numbers: integers, fixed-point fractions, floating-point fractions, double-precision fractions, complex numbers, vectors of the above kinds. The truth values are only 1 bit. Clearly, the stack must be able to hold the largest number you expect to use. Less clear is how you should distinguish among various kinds of numbers.

One way is to define separate operations for each kind of number:

+ integer and fixed-point add (they are the same).

+F floating-point add.

+D double-precision add.

Another is to make a stack entry long enough to contain a code identifying the kind of number. This makes the code defining each operation more elaborate and raises the problem of illegal arguments. I recommend not checking arguments and defining separate operations, for reasons of simplicity. Actually, you are working with one kind of number at a time and the problem may never arise.

Do not bother with mixed-mode arithmetic. You never *need* it, and it's not convenient often enough to be worth the great bother. With multiple word numbers (complex, double-precision) you may put the address of the number on the stack. However, this leads to 3-address operations with the result generally replacing one of the arguments. And this, in turn, leads to complications about constants.

In general, the number of things you *might* do with numbers increases indefinitely. Many of these are mutually incompatible. Basic Principle!

4.4 Definition entries

I must now describe an entry more complicated than any so far, though not the most complicated that you'll see. It is also exceptional in that it's not optional. For this ability is required for any effective application language: to be able to define one word in terms of others. To abbreviate, if you will. You recall that I characterised words as being simple in themselves, but powerful in combination. Well here is a way to combine words.

A definition consists of a defining entry ":" followed by a series of words terminated by ";". The intention is that the word defined by ":" has the meaning expressed by the words that follow. For example:

: ABS DUP 0 LESS IF MINUS THEN ;

This is a definition of the word ABS. Its purpose is to take the absolute value of the number on the stack. It does this by executing a series of words that have the proper effect.

You may consider this a rather clumsy definition of ABS. Especially since there is an instruction on your computer that does exactly that. you're quite right, definitions tend to be clumsy. But they let us use words that we hadn't the foresight to provide entries for. Given certain basic words we can construct any entry we need. Definitions provide a succinct distinction between a control language and an application language: The control language must have all its capabilities built in; the application language can construct those capabilities it needs.

To implement definitions is simple, yet awkwardly subtle. The parameter field of a definition contains the addresses of the dictionary entries that define it. You must somehow deposit these entries in the parameter area, and later fetch them when you execute the definition. The complementary processes of definition and execution are more involved than for any other entry we've encountered.

Before I describe these processes in detail, let me try to clarify exactly what a definition is. You recall that the code executed for a word is a routine, and not a subroutine. And yet a series of words is like a series of subroutine calls, for the control loop serves the function of returning to a position where the next word can be found. You might consider a definition to be just that: a series of subroutine calls with the addresses of the subroutines constituting the definition.

Another viewpoint is concealed in an abbreviation I use: I speak of "executing a word", when I really mean executing the code associated with the word. Or even more precisely, executing the code whose address is stored in the dictionary entry for the word. The abbreviation is not only convenient, it suggests that a word is an instruction that can be executed. And indeed, it is helpful to think of a word as an instruction: an instruction for a computer that is being simulated by our real computer. Let's call that imaginary computer the "virtual computer". Thus, when you type words you are presenting instructions to the virtual computer. The control loop becomes the instruction fetch circuitry of the virtual computer.

If we extend this analogy to definitions, a definition becomes a subroutine for the virtual computer. And the process of defining a definition is equivalent to compiling this subroutine. We'll return to this analogy later.

You'll see that the virtual computer is a real help in understanding definitions. In fact, it originally led me to apply compiler techniques to definitions - techniques that otherwise wouldn't have occurred to me. But although it may be helpful to programmers, it is only confusing to non-programmers. So, I prefer the name "definition" for this type of entry, and the phrase "defining one word in terms of others" as its explanation.

Definitions are extremely powerful. Why, is hard to explain, hard even to comprehend. Their value is best appreciated by hindsight. You complete a ludicrously simple implementation of an application, discover that you used a dozen definitions and nested them 8 deep. The definitions appear responsible for the simplicity.

But there are several properties that emphasize the value of definitions over their equivalent, a series of subroutine calls. First, you needn't be concerned about call sequence, about what registers are available and what must be saved; simply type a word. Second, one definition can execute another. That is, you can nest definitions, again without any concern about saving return addresses or other register conflicts. You can even use definitions recursively without concern. Third, you can pass arguments among definitions effortlessly, in fact invisibly, since they are on the stack. Again, you have no concern for calling sequence or storage conflicts. Plenty of temporary storage is available, too; again, on the stack.

Of course, you have to pay for this convenience, though probably less than you would with FORTRAN subroutine calls. The price is the control loop. It's pure overhead. Executing the code for each entry of course proceeds at computer speed; however, obtaining the address of the next code to execute takes some instructions, about 8. This is why I urge you to optimize your control loop.

Notice that if the code executed for words is long compared to the control loop, the cost is negligible. This is the principle of control languages. As the code shrinks to control loop size, and smaller, overhead rises to 50% and higher. This is the price of an application language. Note, however, that 50% overhead is easily reached with operating systems and compilers that support an application program.

I suggest that you compromise. Code the computation-limited portions of your problem and use definitions for the rest. The use of definitions to control, rather than perform, calculations is inexpensive. And the ease of constructing them reduces the time and effort, and thus cost, of implementation.

4.4.1 Defining a definition

The defining entry ":" acts just like any other. It passes the address EXECUTE to the ENTRY subroutine. I'll discuss that code in the next section.

It then sets a switch STATE. The control loop must be changed to test STATE: if it is 0, words are executed as I've already described; if it is 1, words are compiled. Let me repeat: if you add definitions to your program, you must modify the control loop so that it will either execute or compile words. If you plan to include definitions from the start, you should plan the control loop accordingly. Implement the switch so that executing words is as fast a possible; you'll execute many more words than you'll compile.

To compile a word is simple. After finding it in the dictionary, you have the address of its dictionary entry. Deposit this address in the parameter field. Notice 2 things: we already have a mechanism for depositing words in the dictionary. ENTRY uses it as well as many defining entries for parameters. The dictionary pointer DP identifies the next available word in the dictionary. All you must do to compile a word is to store its address at DP and advance DP. Also notice that we deposit the address of the *entry* not the address of the code executed. This is so we have access not only to the code but also to the parameter field, and even the word itself should we need it.

All right, so much for compiling words. What about numbers? A number presented to a compiler is called a literal. And literals are a problem to any compiler. Fortunately, we can define our virtual computer so that it can handle literals in-line. You must again modify the control loop to test STATE when a number is successfully converted.

Before showing how to compile a number, let me define pseudo-entries. A pseudo-entry is a dictionary entry that is not in the dictionary. That is, it has the format of an entry, but it is not linked to other entries. Thus, it would never be found during a dictionary search. You see, we occassionally need entries to permit the virtual computer to run smoothly, but we don't want to slow the dictionary search by including non-referencable entries.

As you've probably guessed, in order to compile a literal, you compile a pseudo-entry. You then follow it by the number itself; that is, you compile the number also. The result is a double-length virtual-computer instruction. The code executed for the pseudo-entry must fetch the number and place it onto the stack. Thus, literals that are compiled have the same effect, when executed, as if they were executed immediately.

Notice that if you have different-size literals, you'll need different pseudo-entries for them And, having brought up the subject, let me discuss word length a moment. Word length for the virtual computer should be about 12 bits. This is because each instruction is composed of simply a dictionary address and 12 bits is enough to identify one of perhaps 1000 entries. If your real computer word length is longer than 18 bits you should pack several virtual-computer instructions into one word. This is possibly awkward, since you must modify DP to address other than a real computer word. But you'll save a lot of space.

Incidently, since literals require extra space when compiled, you might define commonly used literals as words:

1 CONSTANT 1

Recall that numbers may be words, since the dictionary is searched before numeric conversion is attempted. And a word requires only a single-length virtual-computer instruction. On the other hand, a dictionary entry takes much more space than a compiled literal, so watch the trade-off.

The code in the control loop that compiles words much watch for ";". It is compiled as usual, but it also resets STATE to prevent further compiling. It also performs another task, which requires a digression.

Notice that when we're compiling a definition we're searching the dictionary for each word. If we reference the word we've just defined, we'll find it. Thus, we'll have made a recursive reference. If you want recursive definitions, fine. However, it's extrememly convenient to exchange recursion for re-definition. That is, to understand a reference to itself inside a definition to refer to an earlier definition.

For example:

```
: = SWAP = ;
```

Here I redefine the = verb to operate upon arguments in the opposite order. I could use a different word for that purpose, but = has mnemonic significance.

In any case, the capability is easy to provide. Let ":" bugger the search so the latest entry cannot be found. And let ";" unbugger the search and thereby activate the new definition. If you want recursive definitions, you could provide a defining entry ":R" that did not bugger, providing you make ";" work for both. I'll mention another technique later.

4.4.2 Executing a definition

I named the code executed for a definition EXECUTE. It must modify the instruction-fetch circuitry of the virtual computer. Recall the structure of the control loop: the routine $NEXT_W$ provides the address of a dictionary entry; the routine associated with this entry is entered; it ultimately returns to $NEXT_W$. The same procedure is required in order to execute a definition, with the exception that $NEXT_W$ is replaced by $NEXT_I$. Where $NEXT_W$ read a word and found it in the dictionary, $NEXT_I$ simply fetches the next entry from the parameter field of the definition.

Thus, you need a variable that identifies the routine to be entered for the next entry. One implementation is to define a field NEXT that contains either the address of $NEXT_W$ or $NEXT_I$. If you jump indirect to NEXT, you will enter the appropriate routine. One task of EXECUTE is therefore to store the address of $NEXT_I$ into NEXT, causing subsequent entries to be obtained in a different way.

Of course, $NEXT_I$ must know where to find the next entry. Here the virtual computer analogy is extended by the addition of an instruction counter. If you define a field, preferably an index register, named IC it can act exactly like an instruction counter on a real computer. It identifies the next entry to be executed and must be advanced during execution.

You can now see the complete operation of $NEXT_I$: fetch the entry identified by IC, advance IC to the next enty, and return to the same point $NEXT_W$ does to execute the entry (or compile it, as the case may be). If you use definitions at all, you'll use them extensively. So $NEXT_I$ should be optimized at the cost of $NEXT_W$. In particular, the code that executes (compiles) entries should be fallen into from NEXT$_I$ and jumped to from NEXT$_W$. This saves one instruction (a jump) in the control loop using NEXT$_I$. This can be 20% of the loop, apart from actually executing the entry's code, for a substantial saving.

Now let's return to EXECUTE. Clearly, in addition to establishing NEXT$_I$ it must initialize IC. But first it must save IC. The process is analogous to a virtual-computer subroutine call. The obvious place to save IC is the return stack. Although it is used for other purposes, none of these conflict with such use. If one definition is executed from within another, it is clear the current IC must be saved. Otherwise the current value of IC is undefined.

One more routine is involved in this process. The code executed for ";" must return from the definition. This means simply that it must restore IC from the return stack. However, it must also restore the value of NEXT, which was set to NEXT$_I$ by EXECUTE. You might store the old value of NEXT in the return stack and let ";" recover it. Simpler, perhaps, is to let the undefined value of IC be zero, and act as a flag to restore NEXT to NEXT$_W$. For while executing definitions, NEXT will always contain NEXT$_I$. Only when returning from a definition that originated within the source text must NEXT$_W$ be reestablished. Since while executing source text IC is irrelevant, it might as well by useful in this limited way.

That's all there is to it. The combination of EXECUTE, NEXT$_I$ and ";" provide a powerful and efficient subroutine facility. Notice that the code "executed" for a definition might actually be compiled, depending on the field STATE, as dicussed earlier. Notice also that the entries executed by a definition might compile other entries. That is, one entry might deposit numbers in the dictionary, using

DP. Thus, although the fields IC and DP are similar in use, DP deposits entries and IC fetches them, they may both be in use at the same time. If you're short of index registers, don't try to combine them.

4.4.3 Conditions

Let me review briefly the process of defining a definition: The word ":" sets a switch that modifies the control loop; it will now compile words instead of executing them. The word ";" is compiled, but also causes the switch to be reset, ending the process of compilation. Following words will now be executed as usual.

We can thus view ";" as being an exceptional word, for it is - in a sense - executed during compilation, at which time it resets that switch. Of course, it is also executed during execution of the definition, with a different effect: it resets IC.

There are other words like ";" that must be executed during compilation. These words control the compilation. They perform code more complicated that simply depositing an entry address. In particular, they are required to provide forward and backward branching.

Rather than talk abstractly about a difficult and subtle point, I'll give some examples of words that I've found useful. As always, you are free to choose your own conventions, but they will probably resemble mine in their basic effects.

Define the words IF, ELSE and THEN to permit the following conditional statement format:

```
boolean value IF true statement ELSE false statement
THEN continue
```

The words have a certain mnemonic value, though they are permuted from the familiar ALGOL format. Such a statement can only appear in a definition, for IF, ELSE and THEN are instruction-generating words.

At definition time, the word IF is executed. It compiles a forward jump. Now I must sidetrack the discussion and define jumps. A jump instruction for the virtual computer is similar to a literal. An in-line literal is a double-length instruction. The code executed for the pseudo-entry comprising the first half, uses the second half as a parameter. Likewise, for jumps: a pseudo-entry uses an in-line parameter to change the virtual-computer instruction-counter (IC). This parameter is the amount, positive or negative, to be added to IC: positive for a forward jump, negative for a backward jump. It is a relative jump address, and the whole construction is used by some real computers.

Actually, we need 2 jump pseudo-entries: a conditional jump and an unconditional jump. The conditional jump jumps only if the stack is non-zero, and it is a destructive operation (its argument is dropped).
All right, back to IF. At definition time it compiles the conditional jump pseudo-entry, followed by a 0. For it doesn't know how far to jump. And it places the location of the 0, the unknown address, onto the stack. Remember that the stack is currently not in use, because we're defining. Later it wil be used by those words we're defining, but at the moment we're free to use it to help in the process.

Now look at ELSE. At definition time it compiles an unconditional jump pseudo-entry followed by 0. But then it stores the current value of DP, the next available location, into the location on the stack. Thus, it provides the distance for the conditional jump generated by IF. Actually, it must subtract to get a relative address, but the principle is clear. In turn it leaves the location of its address on the stack.

Finally, we come to THEN. It fixes-up the address that ELSE left dangling. That is, it subtracts the stack from DP and stores the result indirectly in the stack; and destructively. Thus, the combination of IF, ELSE and THEN use the stack to construct forward jump virtual-computer instructions. Since ELSE and THEN act identically in fixing-up the missing address, ELSE can be omitted without any modification. Also, since the stack is used to store unfulfilled jumps, IF . . . THEN statements may be nested. The only restriction is that all addresses are determined; that is, that all locations are removed from the stack. This will be the case if every IF has a matching THEN; ELSE is always optional.

Of course, there's nothing unusual about this technique. All compilers generate forward jumps in this manner. What is somewhat unusual is applying it to the compilation of instructions for a virtual-computer. But it seems to be the best way.

Let's consider a related construction. Very often we are faced with logical expressions that consist of a string of ANDs or a string of ORs. The truth value of such expressions may be determined before the entire expression is evaluated. You can save time by quitting once you know the final result. For example, consider the statement:

```
a b AND c AND IF . . . THEN
```

where a, b, c are boolean expressions; and the statement would read in ALGOL

```
if a and b and c then . . .
```

If a is false, we might as well quit, since the disjunction cannot possibly be true. If you re-write the statement as:

```
a IF b IF c IF . . . THEN THEN THEN
```

the effect is the same; if a, b and c are all true the conditional statement is executed. Otherwise not. Each IF generates a forward jump that is caught by its matching THEN. Note that you must still match IFs with THENs. In fact, this is one sort of nested IF . . . THEN statement. It is an extremely efficient construction.

Now consider the corresponding statement with ORs:

```
a b OR c OR IF . . . THEN
```

or in ALGOL

```
if a or b or c then
```

If a is true you may as well quit, for the conjunction cannot be false. If you re-write the statement as

```
a -IF b -IF c IF HERE HERE . . . THEN
```

and if you define

```
: HERE SWAP THEN ;
```

    : -IF NOT IF ;

the statement works as follows: if a is true, -IF will jump; if b is true, -if will jump; if c is false, IF will jump. The first HERE will catch b's jump (the SWAP gets c's address out of the way); the second HERE catches a's jump; THEN catches c's jump. Thus, a and b jump into the condition, while c jumps over it.

This is a slightly clumsy statement, but I've found no simpler solution. If you used them regularly, you'd doubtless acquire facility, and it would seem quite natural. Just watch that you match all IFs. Moreover, the same technique could be applied to more complex logical expressions - with even greater clumsiness.

4.4.4 Loops

I'll continue with a couple more examples of words executed at definition time. This time examples of backward jumps, used to construct loops.
Consider the pair of words BEGIN and END, as used in a statement like:

BEGIN . . . boolean END

BEGIN stores DP onto the stack, thus marking the beginning of a loop. END generates a conditional backward jump to the location left by BEGIN. That is, it deposits a conditional jump pseudo-entry, subtracts DP+1 from the stack, and deposits that relative address. If the boolean value is false during execution, you stay in the loop. When it becomes true, you exit.

BEGIN and END provide a loop terminated by a logical condition. Let's define another loop. This one counts an index through a range to control the looping:

a b DO . . . CONTINUE

a and b represent arguments on the stack. DO acts just like BEGIN. CONTINUE requires a new pseudo-entry that tests the top 2 words on the stack for equality and jumps if they are unequal. During compilation CONTINUE deposits this pseudo-entry and then computes the jump distance as did END. Thus, CONTINUE uses another conditional jump: one that tests the stack for equal, instead of for false. It is also a non-destructive operation, so long as its arguments are unequal. When they become equal and terminate the loop, it drops them.

Presumably, inside the DO . . . CONTINUE loop the arguments are modified so as to terminate the loop. This can be done many ways. For example, to run the loop from 1 to 10:

10 0 DO 1 + . . . CONTINUE

The first argument is 10, the stopping value; the second is 0, which is immediately incremented to 1, the index value. Within the loop this index is available for use. The DUP operation will obtain a copy. Each time through the loop the index will be incremented by 1. After the loop is executed for index value 10, the CONTINUE operation will stop the loop and drop the 2 arguments - now both 10.

Alternatively, the same loop could be written:

11 1 DO . . . 1 + CONTINUE

Here the index is incremented at the end of the loop, instead of the beginning. Upon reaching 11 and exceeding the limit of 10, the loop is stopped.

Naturally loops can be counted backwards, or indeed many other methods of modifying the index used. It will always terminate on equality. Of course, such a flexible loop control runs the risk of never stopping at all. If you increment the index incorrectly, it will happily run forever. But used carefully, it's a convenient tool.

A refinement of DO . . . CONTINUE is not difficult. If the arguments are equal to start with, DO can generate a conditional forward jump that CONTINUE will fix-up. Thus, you may do a loop *no* times. However, such loops are the exception; but if you encounter one, you'll find the conditional statement required to protect it most awkward.

4.4.5 Implementation

I hope you now appreciate the need for words that are executed at define time. I'm sure you're aware of the need for branches and loops. Perhaps you'll notice that I did not mention labels; the branch generating words I mentioned, and others you can invent, are perfectly capable of handling jumps without labels. You saw in the definition of HERE how the stack can be manipulated to permit overlapping jumps as well as nested ones. However, in a sense we have many labels, for every dictionary entry effectively assigns a name to a piece of code.

Now to consider some problems I glossed over. Clearly you must be able to recognize those words that are to be executed during definitions. That is, IF, THEN, BEGIN, END, etc. must somehow override the normal mechanism whereby the control loop would compile them. I mentioned a switch that distinguished execution from compilation. Let's establish a similar flag (1 bit) in each dictionary entry, with the values

1: execute

0: compile

applying both to switch and flag.

For a given entry, 'or' the switch and flag together; if either is 1, execute the word, else compile it.

The above rule is correct, and even fairly efficient. Remember that we want the control loop efficient! And it's adequate providing all words that must be executed are built into your system dictionary.

Unfortunately, it's not adequate for the examples I gave above, which probably means it's inadequate, since those were pretty simple examples. But complication is part of the fun of programming. So, pay attention and I'll try to explain some problems I don't understand very well myself.

Editor: I don't understand my concern about SWAP below. The word ! did not endure. Don't try to reconcile what I said. I can't. Consider the definition of HERE I gave above:

```
: HERE SWAP THEN ;
```

Here is one of those imperative words; it must be executed at definition time. But it is defined as an ordinary definition - and would be compiled. Even if we managed to execute HERE, the first word in its definition is SWAP: a most ordinary word, and one that would certainly be compiled, except that we intend it, too, to be executed. The next word, THEN, offers no problem - or does it? If we can execute HERE we'll also execute THEN, since it's imperative. However, we have a problem at the time we *define* HERE; we'll try to *execute* THEN, when we want to *compile* it. That is, sometimes we want to compile imperative words; and sometimes we want to execute ordinary words - even in a definition.

So, what to do? I bet you think I have a solution. Your faith is touching, but I don't have a very good one. It suffers a small restriction, but a nagging one: you may not execute a literal in a definition. To phrase it positively: literals must be compiled inside definitions. Let's see how it works.

Consider the switch STATE. It's normally 0; ":" makes it 1 to indicate compilation. Let's define a new defining entry ":!" that acts exactly like ":" with 2 exceptions:

It sets the entry flag to 1; to mark an imperative word.

It sets STATE to 2; to force all words to be compiled. Since the test in the control loop is to execute if STATE and flag are equal, nothing will execute.

";" is unchanged; its sets STATE to 0 for both sorts of definitions. This solves all our problems except SWAP. How do we execute words that ordinarily would be compiled?

Define a new entry "!". Let it execute the last entry compiled and remove it from the compilation. Now we can re-write the definition of HERE as

```
: ! HERE SWAP ! THEN ;
```

and it will work. I'll review the rules:

All words are normally executed.

Only words flagged imperative are executed in definitions.

Any word can be made imperative by following it with an "!".

A definition can be made imperative by using ":!" instead of ":" to define it.

Now the restriction I mentioned should be apparant. A literal cannot be made imperative with a "!" because it's a double-length instruction - and the "!" code has no way of knowing that. Oh well, we could set a field to indicate the length of the last compiled instruction, but it's not that great a problem. Besides, in that case successive !s wouldn't work.

4.5   Code entries

I've explained definitions and how they, in effect, compile instructions for the virtual-computer. What about compiling code for your real computer then? Of course, you can. But you probably won't.

The Basic Principle intrudes. If you add code entries to your program, you add enormous power and flexibility. Anything your computer can do, any instructions it has, any tricks you can play with its hardware are at you fingertips. This is fine, but you rarely need such power. And the cost is appreciable. You'll need many entries (say 10) to provide a useful compiler; plus all the instruction mnemonics. Moreover, you'll have to design an application language directed at the problem of compiling code.

I don't want to down-grade the possibility or value of such efforts, but you wrote your program in some language to start with. If you need additional code it's much easier to re-compile your program and add what you need. Only if you have an application that needs tailored code. or can profit by providing different code to different users, or different code at different times, can you satisfy the Basic Principle.

On the other hand, if you start with code entries, you can construct all the other entries I've been talking about: arithmetic operators, noun entries, definitions. In Chapter 9 I'll show how you can use code entries in a really essential role; and achieve a significantly more efficient and powerful program than by any other means. But except for that I'm afraid they are marginal.

So how can you generate code? First you need a defining entry that defines a code entry. The characteristic of a code entry is that it executes code stored in its parameter field. Thus, the address passed to ENTRY by its defining entry (say CODE) must be the location into which will be placed the first instruction. This is not DP, because the entry itself takes space; but is simply DP plus a constant.

Second you need an entry to deposit a number at DP. We have used such a routine several times, constructing variables and definitions, but we've not had an entry for it. I suggest the word "," although that might conflict with your output entries. All it does is move a number from the stack to the parameter field. Instructions are numbers of course. You'll construct them on the stack and then deposit them. Incidently, this is a useful entry - apart from compiling code. You'll find it useful for initializing data arrays of all kinds.

Now you can appreciate the source of my earlier caution. You'll have to provide a flock of entries that access code compiled into your program that we've not needed to reference directly before. For example, RETURN: when your routine is finished, it must jump to the control loop, just as your built-in entries do. However, you don't know the location of the control loop in core; and it moves as you change your program. So, you must have an entry to generate a RETURN instruction.

Likewise, if you plan to compile defining entries you must provide entries that will generate subroutine calls to ENTRY. Other code might want to access WORD or NUMBER or indeed any facility already available in your program. Moreover, you will have to define variable entries for those fields you will use: D and F for output;

perhaps STATE and BASE; Basically, the problem is that you must make available outside your program, all the labels available inside it already. You must use them enough to justify the effort.

All right, you've done that much. Now you've got to decide how to construct an instruction. They have several fields - instruction, index, adddress - that you'll want to put onto the stack separately and combine somehow. This is easy to do, but hard to design. You probably don't want to copy your assembler, and probably couldn't follow its format conveniently anyway. In fact, you can do a good job of designing a readable compiler language; but it will take some effort. Definitions provide all the tools you need.

For example, you might write a definition that will "or" together an instruction and address and deposit it. Or if your hardware's awkward, you can provide a definition that converts absolute addresses to relative or supplies appropriate paging controls. Whatever you need or want can be readily defined. Done properly, such a compiler is a substantial application in itself, and if you're going to do it at all, plan to spend the necessary time and effort.

We discussed conditional statements and loops for the virtual computer. Precisely the same techniques apply here, with due allowance for hardware variations. In fact, I originally applied the stack-oriented branch generation to code for my real computer. Such statements are really the difference between an assembler and a compiler. Keep in mind the Basic Principle.

One valuable use of a compiler is the permit the definition of new kinds of nouns. That is, to construct new defining entries. As an example, consider using the primitive compiler to define instruction entries as described just above. Or you might want to define entries that multiply the top of the stack by a constant.

As usual when adding an ability, several distinct entries must cooperate to provide it. In this case ENTER and ;CODE. Let me illustrate:

```
: UNIT ENTER , ;CODE 1 V LDA , SP MPY , SP STA , NEXT ,

2.54 UNIT IN

4. IN
```

The first line defines the word UNIT. The next line uses this defining entry to define the word IN (inches). The last line uses IN in a way that puts 4 inches onto the stack, as centimeters. The 3 lines are equivalent to

```
: IN 2.54 * ;
```

which is certainly simpler. But if you want to define many UNITs, a special defining entry is much more convenient and efficient.

The first special word is ENTER. It calls the ENTRY subroutine used by all your defining entries, but passes a 0 address as the location of the code to be executed. Look at the definition of UNIT. The word ENTER is imperative. It generates a double-length pseudo-instruction; a pseudo-entry for the first half and a 0 constant for the second. At execution time, the pseudo-entry will call ENTRY to construct a new dictionary entry, passing the following constant as the address of code to be executed. The word ;CODE is a combination of the words ";" and CODE. It terminates the definition of UNIT and stores DP into the address field established by ENTER. Thus the code that follows ;CODE is the code that will be executed for all entries created by UNIT. ;CODE knows where to store DP because ENTER is restricted to being the first word in any definition that uses it; and ;CODE knows which definition it is terminating.

The restriction on the position of ENTER is unimportant, it may as well be first as anywhere else. In the case of UNIT, only a "," to deposit the constant was needed. Other nouns might need more elaborate processing to establish their parameter field.

You notice I gave an example of code following ;CODE. You see instruction mnemonics and addresses deposited by ",". I don't want to explain this compiler language, for it is not relevant for your computer.

One more suggestion might prove helpful. You might define a new kind of constant: an instruction. When executed, an instruction expects an address on the stack, extracts a constant from its parameter field and constrcts and deposits a completed instruction. You'll probably have a large number of instructions and use a large number. This will save you many deposit entries.

I'm sorry, but I think it's infeasible to attempt an example. If you can't see how to construct your own code entries from what I've already said, forget it. The application is extremely machine dependent - and rightly so. Don't attempt to apply the same code to several computers; definitions already do that for you. The purpose of code is to exploit the properties of your particular computer.

5. Programs with memory

You may perhaps grant the value of a program that grows, without being willing to provide the volume of input required. Naturally it does little good to have a hundred dictionary entries if you must type every one. Obviously, we need a place to save entries and obviously that place is disk (or drum, or other random secondary memory).

What is not obvious is how to store entries. It ought to be a Second Principle that you never save anything on disk without being able to modify it, but this rule is universally ignored. To simply copy dictionary entries violates another cardinal principle: never store core address on disk. You could never modify your program without chasing down all code addresses.

Fortunately, there is a solution. Store on disk the text from which dictionary entries are constructed. It is a simple matter to divert the input routine from reading your message buffer to reading disk. This chapter will show how.

5.1 Organization of disk

There is only one way to organize disk. In the same way that core is divided into a large number of words, disk must be divided into a large number of blocks. In the same way that words are the smallest field that can be fetched from core, blocks are the smallest field that can be fetched from disk. A block contains 256 words.

A block contains 256 words because that is the size of a 1-byte address, and because 256 4-byte words hold 1024 bytes which is the amount of text that can be displayed on a typical scope.

However, here is another instance in which your application and hardware must play a dominant role. Disks usually have a hardware block-size that offers advantages. You must choose a multiple of that. Your application may involve storing data on disk, and you must choose a block size useful for data as well as text. I say no less than 512 characters nor more than 1024. 128-word blocks have recently been mentioned; fine if the words are 6 or 3 bytes (characters).

5.1.1 Getting blocks

In trying to anticipate the organization of a random file, certain principles are obvious. Cross-references between blocks will probably be wanted. Such references are simple if they use absolute block addresses; extremely clumsy otherwise. We may use absolute addresses if we promise never to move a block. This means we can never pack disk. We agree cheerfully because we didn't want to pack disk anyway.

This means that as the data in blocks becomes useless, space will become available in block-sized holes. We must somehow re-use these holes. Which means that we must allocate, and re-allocate, disk in block-sized pieces.

All addresses start at 0, block addresses included (otherwise you find youself forever adding and subtracting 1). However, we cannot use block 0 - for anything. You will find that most addressing errors involve block 0. If you look at block 0 from time to time you will find the most amazing things there. You will find block 1 a useful place to store things you need to remember from run to run. Like the address of the first block available for re-use - none: 0. And the address of the last block used - initially: 1.

You will want to copy disk (onto another disk, or tape) for protection. You need only copy the nuber of blocks used, which is usually less than half the disk capacity, or else you're pretty worried about space. If you destroy block 1 (you will) you will have to re-load the entire disk from your back-up. Never try to recover just block 1, you'll end up horribly confused.

You may want to put your object program on this disk. Fine! It won't even take many blocks. You may need to start it in block 0 in order to do an initial load (bootstrap). OK, but be able to re-load the program (only) from back-up because you will destroy block 0. Only if you destroy the block (we'll call it block 1) containing available space information must you re-load data (all data). Unless you destroy many blocks. Choose the path of least confusion, not least effort. Re-loading disk will confuse you, you'll forget what you've changed and be days discovering it. Much better you spend hours re-typing text and re-entering data.

So, when you need a block, you type a word (GET) which reads block 1, places the block up for re-use on the stack, reads that block, places the contents of its first word into block 1, and re-writes block 1. The first word, of course, contains the address of the next block up for re-use. If no block was availabe for re-use (initially the case), GET increments the last block used, puts it on the stack and re-writes block 1. GET then clears your new block to 0 and re-writes it.

Several comments: Notice that GET places its result on the stack - the logical place where it is available for further use. Notice that blocks are re-used in preference to expanding the disk used. This makes sense except for the problem of arm motion. Forget arm motion. You just have to live with it. This is, after all, a random memory. Don't neglect clearing the block to 0.

5.1.2 Releasing blocks

To release a block, put it on the stack and say RELEASE. It will read block 1, extract the next block for re-use, place the stack there and write block 1; then read the released block and place the old next-block in the first word. All we're doing, of course, in constructing the chain of available blocks used by GET. Possibly the block you release is linked to other blocks. You must release all those, too. A convenient way is to use the first word as a link field. Then the available block chain is the same as any other block chain. To concatenate chains, you place the first block in block 1, run down the chain to the last block (0 in link) and place the old next-block in that link.

Don't be tempted to maintain a count of the available blocks. Its not worth the trouble. If you must know, you can count the length of the available chain.

If you have enough different kinds of blocks, it may be useful to store a code identifying the block in the first word (or second). You can then examine all blocks of a certain kind. Available blocks should have code 0.

How many blocks you can have is probably limited by the disk, however it may be limited by the field you choose to store block addresses in. Be careful! You can circumvent the first limit by modifying your read subroutine to choose one of several disks. You must re-format all your block addresses (cross-references on disk, remember) to expand the second.

5.1.3 Reading and writing disk

I'm sure you know how to read disk. However, do not choose a block size that causes the slightest difficulty: like half a block between tracks. If you check the GET routine, you'll see that you'll need 2 blocks in core at once. This is a reasonable minimum, it makes it easy to move things from one block to another. However, you'll have lots of core left over and you might as well use it for buffering disk; especially if access time is noticeable.

You'll want a table specifying which blocks are in core: your read routine can check this table before reading.

But you should not write a block when you change it. Rather mark it 'to be written' in the buffer table. When you come to re-use that buffer, write the old block first. The principle is that you're likely to change a block again if you change it once. If you minimize writes you can save a lot of disk accesses. Of course, there is a trade-off - if your program crashes, you may have updated blocks in core that aren't on disk. You should be able to re-start your program and preserve the core buffers.

Of course, multiple core buffers imply an allocation problem. A simple round-robin is as effective a scheme as any.

If you are going to scan data sequentially, you can save many accesses by reading consecutive blocks at the same time. However, it is likely that random reads may be interspersed with these sequential ones. An effective solution is to store the *last* block in the sequential area and the number of blocks somewhere for your read subroutine. If the block isn't in core, and is within the sequential range, it can read as many consecutive blocks as there are consecutive buffers available. Don't attempt more than this - ie, making more buffers available. The net effect is that you will do the best you can with sequential blocks, subject to interfering constraints.

You will inevitably spend a lot of effort reading-writing disk. But remember the Basic Principle!

5.2 Text on disk

You will store a lot of text on disk - hundreds of blocks - but this is probably a small fraction of your disk. The rest is presumably data for your application(s).

A block that contains text (I mean text to be read and executed by your program) contains one long character string. If the first word contains control information, it starts in the second word and extends until a particular word marks the end (perhaps ;S). This end word is important because it is inconvenient to have the input routine test for end-of-block. You quickly learn not to leave that word out.

A block that contains text should have a special name, for you will be using it often in conversation. I have called such blocks SHEETs - since the text filled a sheet of paper - and SCREENs - since the text filled the screen of a scope. Define the word READ to save the input address, the block and character position of the next character to be scanned, on the return stack; and reset the input pointer to the block on the stack and the first character position. Define the word ;S to restore the original input pointer. Very simply you can have your program read block 123:

`123 READ`

However . . . there's always a however, isn't there. You must modify your word routine to read the current block before scanning. This is expensive but essential (of course no actual read is performed if the block is in core), for the last word executed may have caused a block to be read that overlaid the block the word was read from. This can especially occur if one screen directs the reading of others (as they will). No other solution to this problem has been satisfactory, so swallow the code - which need not be great.

You will find that with text on disk, the original characterization of 'input' as low volume is strained. You will read many words and do many dictionary searches. However, on a microsecond computer, you won't notice it.

5.2.1 Text editing

Never put anything on disk you can't modify! And we haven't discussed how you get text on disk in the first place. Do not load it from cards! You're misdirecting your effort toward card reading, and you had to punch the cards anyway. Type it. The definitions required to edit the text stored in blocks (SCREENs) is simple.

You must be able to handle character strings surrounded with quotes (4.1). Given that, I shall exhibit a text editing screen. This is a simple example of the value of definitions. You may notice it is the first non-trivial exmple I've given. You should be motivated by now to give it proper attention.

Naturally, you're going to have to type these definitions twice. Once to put them into your dictionary; again, to use them to put them in a screen (bootstrapping). In fact you'll probably type them many times, but 2 is minimum.

I'm going to exhibit an annotated copy of the EDIT screen I used in a particular program. It uses system entries whose value may not be clear. They are borrowed from other aspects of the application.

```
0 C1 42 # :R RECORD
```

Here I am constructing a field description: RECORD is a 42 character field starting in character 1 of word 0 of the current block (understood). I'm using blocks that can hold 15 42-character lines; a word has 6 characters, so that's 15 7-word lines.

```
: LINE 1 - 7 * RECORD + ;
```

Here I'm defining a verb that will convert a line number (1-15) to a field address. It modifies the RECORD descriptor by changing the word specification (low order bits). Thus line 1 starts in word 0; line 2 in word 7; etc.

```
: T CR LINE ,C ;
```

If I type 3 T - I want line 3 typed. T does a carriage return (CR), executes LINE to compute the field address, and copies the (character) field into the message buffer (,C).

```
: R LINE =C ;
```

If I type " NEW TEXT" 6 R - I want line 6 to be replaced by the text in quotes. The leading quote puts a string descriptor on the stack. R then executes LINE, followed by =C to store the quote string in the field. The block will automatically be re-written, since it was changed.

```
: LIST 15 0 DO 1 +

CR DUP LINE ,C DUP ,I CONTINUE ;
```

LIST will list the entire block: 15 42-character lines followed by line numbers. It sets up a DO-CONTINUE loop with the stack varying from 1 - 15. Each time through the loop it: does a CR; copies the stack and executes LINE; types the field (,C); copies the stack again and types it as an integer (,I).

```
: I 1 + DUP 15 DO 1 -
```

```
DUP LINE DUP 7 + =C CONTINUE R ;
```

If I type " NEW TEXT" 6 I - I want the text inserted after line 6. "I" must first shift lines 7 - 14 down one position (losing line 15) and then replace line 7. It adds 1 to the line number, sets up a backwards DO-CONTINUE loop starting at 14, constructs two field descriptors, LINE and LINE+7, and shifts them (,C). When the loop if finished, it does an R.

```
: D 15 SWAP DO 1 +

DUP LINE DUP 7 - =C CONTINUE " " 15 R ;
```

If I type 12 D - I want to delete line 12. D must move lines 13-15 up one position and clear line 15: It sets up a DO-CONTINUE loop from stack+1 to 15. Each iteration it: constructs fields LINE and LINE-7 and shifts them (=C). Then it replaces line 15 with spaces.

That's it. With 10 lines of code I can define a text-editor. It's not the most efficient possible, but it's fast enough and illustrates many points: In dealing with small amounts of text, you needn't be clever; let the machine do the work.

The verb LINE is an extremely useful one; such useful verbs are invariably an empirical discovery. The verbs ,C and =C are the heart of the method; incidently, they only work on fields less than 64 characters. Notice how one definition wants to reference another (R used by I and D; LINE used by all). Notice how I and D are similar yet different. And notice how a few verbs eliminate a lot of bookkeeping and let you concentrate on the problem and not the details.

6.   Programs with output

By now I'm sure you're aware that the heart of your program is its control loop. It not only controls the operation, but also the philosophy and organization of the program. Let me review its operation: it reads a word, finds it in the dictionary and executes its code; failing that it converts it to a binary number and places it onto the stack; failing that it types an error message.

So far, I've ignored that error message; not because it's unimportant or trivial to implement, but because it's part of a diffcult subject - output. Logically I oughtn't have delayed discussing output this long, for even a control language needs output. But as usual in this program it is involved with other features that we've only just discussed. I'll leave it to you to implement those features of the output capabilities I'll present, that your application requires.

Most compilers, and therefore most programmers, regard output the inverse of input. For example, FORTRAN uses the same FORMAT statements for output as for input, thereby suggesting that the two processes are very similar. But are they?

You compose input: you select words and combine them into fairly complex phrases; your program spends considerable effort deciphering this input and extracting its meaning. In reply it will not go through any such elaborate procedure. You'll see that most of its output consists of the word OK. You are talking to the computer, but it is hardly talking to you; at best it's grunting.

I maintain that the two processes have nothing in common, that the computer does not prepare output in a manner analogous to you preparing input. In Chapter 8 I'll describe a way your program can compose complex output messages. Although such a technique might provide a 2-way dialog, it has even less similarity to interpreting input.

6.1 Output routines

You will need 3 output subroutines; conceivably you could get by with 2. One to type a number of spaces. One to type a number of characters from a specified location ($TYPE_N$). One to type characters until it encounters a space ($TYPE_B$) and including the space. This last depends on your dictionary format, for it is used to type entry words. Of course, these should use the fetch and deposit subroutines you use for input.

Let us use the composition of an error message as an example. You have just typed an input message, and the carriage is positioned at the last character. First you want a space. Then use $TYPE_B$ to type the current word. It caused the error and will tell you where it occurred. You don't need this for an unbuffered device. Then use $TYPE_B$ again to type a word that describes the error. Avoid long error messages - you're the one who will wait while they're typed. You can detect a number of errors, so it's worth your while to devise a routine to generate them.

After finding an error, you of course quit doing whatever you were doing. There is no point in trying to continue when you're standing by ready to correct and start again. However, it is convenient to reset things that you'd probably have to reset anyway. In particular, set the stacks empty. This is sometimes unfortunate since the parameter stack might help you locate an error. But it usually is most convenient. Don't try to reset the dictionary since you're not sure what you may want to reset it to.

6.2 Acknowledgement

I mentioned in Chapter 3 that you must write subroutines to send and receive messages. Now I must expand on exactly how you should use these subroutines.

Recall that input and output share the same message buffer. This now causes trouble. However, it considerably simplifies the more powerful message routines of Chapter 7. On balance the single message buffer seems optimal.

First let me call the subroutine that sends a message SEND. It sends a single line and should add a carriage return to the line, as well as any other control characters needed, and translate characters as required. The routine that receives a message is QUERY. It is a routine, and not a subroutine. QUERY calls SEND to send a message, and then awaits and processes an input message. stripping control characters and translating characters as required. It initializes the input pointer IP and jumps to $NEXT_W$. Notice that your program can send output via SEND wherever it pleases. However, it can only receive input in conjunction with output, via QUERY. You have no provision for receiving successive messages without intervening output. This is exactly the behavior you need, and actually simplifies the coding of message I/O.

Now let me describe the use of QUERY. Each input message is terminated with an end-of-message word, a non-printing character surrounded by spaces. This word has a dictionary entry that types the word OK and jumps to QUERY. Thus, after interpreting each input message, your program types a brief acknowledgement - OK, message received and understood - and awaits further input.

Notice that if an input message generates output it destroys itself. That is, the output is placed in the message buffer irrespective of the input already there. Thus, a word that generates output should be the last word in a message, since succeeding words will not be seen. In particular, the end-of-message word won't be seen, and the reply OK won't be typed. This is what you want: OK is only typed in lieu of any other output.

OK should appear on the same line as the input message, separated from the last word by a least one space. QUERY should not acknowledge receipt of a message - as most time-sharing systems do - with a carriage-return. The only acknowledgement is the OK at completion of interpretation. Placing OK on the same line helps distinguish output from input and compresses the conversation, especially valuable on a limited-size scope face. A user must not type input until he receives output. It's only important to enforce this rule with multi-user programs. For this see Chapter 7.

In order to determine whether there is input in the message buffer, establish a field EMPTY. QUERY should set empty false and each output generating entry should set it true. Actually, output generating verbs have much in common with each other, and each should jump to a routine that does the following:

Drop the stack. Each output verb must have an argument. Its last argument can be dropped at this point, and the stack pointer checked against its lower limit.

Set EMPTY true.

If NEXT contains NEXT$_W$ and SCREEN is 0, jump to QUERY. Under these circumstances there is no further input available in the message buffer.

Jump to NEXT.

Notice that if entries are coming from a definition or from a screen, no conflict can arise with the message buffer. Only if input is currently being read from the message buffer is there a problem.

However, there are 2 places where source of input is changed. This is in the code for ";" and ";S". If ";" restores NEXT$_W$ to NEXT, it must guarantee that input is available. That is, jump to QUERY if EMPTY is true and SCREEN is 0. Likewise, if ";S" restores SCREEN to 0, it should jump to QUERY if EMPTY is true (NEXT is guaranteed to be NEXT$_W$.

The logic required is summarized in Fig 6.2 and is the price paid for duplexing the message buffer. One final complication concerns EMPTY. If true, it states that input has been destroyed; it does not indicate that output is currently in the message buffer. Output may have been placed there and already sent. If the message buffer is empty, type OK before jumping to QUERY.

6.3 Character strings

Everything isn't easy, and this particular feature is my nemesis. Perhaps a measure of its value is the difficulty of its implementation. A character string is an awkward entity. Mostly because there is nowhere to put it. Numeric literals go on the stack in a most natural fashion. Character strings won't fit, and that isn't what we want to do with them anyway.

My solution is this. When you see a character string, leave it alone. Put on the stack a descriptor giving the address of the first charactere and the number of characters in the string. Skip over the string. That is, advance the input pointer to its end. You can't do it in quite that order, of course, because only by skipping can you discover the number of characters.

What does a character string look like? Of all the ways you might choose, one is completely natural:

"ABCDEF . . . XYZ"

A character string is enclosed in quotes. It can contain any character except a quote, specifically including spaces.

We get in trouble immediately! How do you recognize a character string? By the leading quote, for course. But do you modify your word subroutine to recognize that quote? If you do so you may never use a leading quote for any other purpose. Much better that the quote is a word by itself, treated like any other dictionary entry, for it can then be re-defined. But words are terminated by spaces, and I still resist making quote an exception. So let's type character strings:

" ABCDEF . . . XYZ"

The extra space is annoying, but in Chapter 8 I will tell you how to eliminate it without the objections I just raised. So, a character string is started with a quote-space and terminated by a quote.

Remember that we leave the character string alone, merely remembering where it is. We are talking about character strings in the input buffer (so far), and we had better use the string before we destroy it with output or additional input. *When* it is destroyed depends on many things, so the best rule is to use it immediately.

What can you do with a character string? I've only found 2 uses. They are very similar, but part of the frustration of implementing them is to take advantage of the similarity. You can type a string, or you can move it to a character field.

To type a string is easy. Define an entry that uses the descriptor on the stack to set parameters for the $TYPE_N$ subroutine.

To move a string is harder, but still easy. You have 2 descriptors on the stack: on top a field descriptor; below the string descriptor. Set the input and output pointers and do a character move of length the smaller of the 2 field sizes. Space fill the remainder of the destination field. Notice that you mustn't move more characters than you have or will fit. And of course, string descriptors will rarely have the right size. Truncating a string is not an error condition!

If you can do the above, you can also move one character field to another. That is, if you make your character string and field descriptors compatible - which adds to the fun. You might want to prevent moving a field to a string, but than who cares.

The problem is to reconcile all the above requirements. Not really to produce optimum code, but even to produce code that is remotely acceptable in size, speed, restrictions and correct operation.

We've slid into the subject of field descriptors. You might want to type a character field, and of course the same code should work as for string descriptors.

6.4 Field entries

We've talked about the different kinds of numbers you might want, and the different entries these require. However, all these entries dealt with computation. Another kind of entry is useful for more sophisticated output purposes. I call it a field-entry because its most common use is to define a field in a data record.

In addition to the descriptor associated with a variable, a field entry needs additional parameters that specify the output format. It is extremely useful to be able to specify a field width for output once and for all, and then use it automatically on all reports. Also, it is useful to be able to reference the name of the field - which of course is contained in the dictionary entry.

So, a useful convention is that a field entry puts the address of itself - that is the dictionary entry - on the stack. Recall that a variable entry places the address of the variable on the stack. If you want the name of the entry, this address tells you where it is. If you want the format, this address - offset by some constant - tells you where to find it. And if you want the address of the field, you can get that too - a process that is executed automatically for a variable.

These various capabilities require various entries to affect them. You might define:

,NM   - **type out field name.**

F   - **extract field width.**

@F   - **obtain field address.**

Depending (as usual) you might be able to make @F compatible with @. Or make @ automatically work correctly for field entries. You may want to distinguish addresses of variables from address of field entries. This would be analogous to distinguishing different kinds of numbers, and for the same reason - so that the same operations (in this case probably @ and =) will work on all.

Apply the Basic Principle.

7. Programs that share

It is not obvious, but a program organized as we have discussed is ideally suited to handling several users simultaneously. All of the basic problems of interactive processing have been solved by interacting with one user. The organization is such that all data is, or can be, stored in the user's dictionary. To distinguish users merely requires the program recognise the proper dictionary.

Of course, the value of multiple users depends upon the application. There appears to be a correlation between the complexity of an application and the number of potential users. An application that deserves a problem-oriented-language my well be of interest to many users on a continuous basis.

Moreover, once the basic program is available, it is relatively simple to add other, even unrelated, applications. The ability to control your vocabulary by reading screens allows a terminal to be used by different people with absolute minimum effort: each can have a personal screen that will load his dictionary with the vocabulary he wants.

Providing the message traffic from any one terminal is low enough, as is inevitably the case - for we have in effect slowed the computer down to human speed - we can handle a much larger number of terminals than can fit in core, hundreds, by storing inactive users on disk.

However, there is a cost, primarily of assuring that re-entrant programming rules are strictly followed. The additional code required to switch the computer's attention among users and the additional core required for disk buffers and user dictionaries demand that a single user application by de-bugged first. And then the capacity of the computer multiplied with a multiple-user control routine as the demand develops. It is all too easy to get bogged down in the multiple-user controller and never to perfect an application. Or to perfect a multiple-user control and never to find a demand to justify it.

Given a successful single-user application, I will show how it can be expanded to many users. If you plan to take this step, there are certain precautions you should take with your original implementation. But mind the Basic Principle!

7.0.1 Non-user activities

Each user has a position in the ready table to identify his status. The computer examines this table to decide what to do next. You may want to add to the ready table entries not associated with users but representing tasks that must be performed by the computer.

For example, if you have to poll phone lines to acquire input, you want to perform these polls asynchronously with whatever other work you're doing. Since interrupt routines are best kept small, the task of translating character sets, checking parity, distributing messages, etc., should be performed at lower priority. This is easy to do with an entry in the ready table. The interrupt routine sets a message routine "ready" and the computer will process it when possible.

Each such independent activity should have a ready table entry and a (perhaps) small dictionary in which to store its parameters; return address, register contents, etc. in the same format as a user activity. In fact these activities are completely equivalent to users, except that they don't process users. This is significant, for it means they never generate error messages, they must handle their own errors, somehow.

If you haven't already noticed, we're now talking about operating systems. I don't have much more to say on the subject, but there are other asynchronous activities you might want:

A clock to handle the timer interrupt and maintain a time and date in core and disk. It might ready other activities that relinquished control for a fixed time.

A routine to write blocks on disk. Periodically it might scan the block buffers for blocks to copy. (however, writing blocks when the read routine needs a buffer seems simpler.)

Such activities cost little, and usually provide the simplest answer to any asynchronous problem. Mind the Basic Principle, though!

7.0.2 Message handling

If you can read input from one user, you can read input from many. You must get an interrupt that tells you input is available and from whom it comes. You simple direct it to the proper message buffer. Likewise, with output.

It needn't be simple, but it certainly depends on hardware exclusively. If you have to poll terminals, it can become very interesting, indeed. But the problem remains beyond the scope of this book.

If all your users are not core resident, it is better if none of them are. Then any input message can be written into the message buffer area on disk. And all output messages read from disk. The fact that some users might reside in core, causes an unreasonable complication, and the fact that disk access is fast compared to message transmission means that to attempt to save such disk accesses is not efficient.

7.1 User control

The fact that you have several users creates a new problem. Of course, the computer can only process one user at a time (we assume a single processor). But when it's finished with one user, it must switch its attention to another.

When is it finished with one user? Clearly, if a user is awaiting input the computer is finished. We are talking about keyboard input, which will take many seconds to arrive. Similarly, if the user is sending output, the computer may as well stop. Output will take several seconds, especially if an acknowledgement from the device is anticipated. It needn't stop. While sending one message, it could be composing the next. But it's much simpler not to attempt such overlap. If the user is reading disk, the computer can stop.

I want to define a single phrase to cover these situations. I shall say that a user relinquishes control of the processor whenever he does message or disk I/O. This is a voluntary action on his part, and those are the only times he relinquishes control. In particular, there is no time quantum that will take control from him. For this reason: With several users, code must clearly be re-entrant. However, if a user is promised that he will be allowed to finish what he starts, if he will not lose control to someone else except when he relinquishes it, the re-entrant requirements become much less onorous. The program need only be re-entrant across I/O, which can save a lot of bother.

All right, what happens when a user relinquishes control? The computer simple scans a table of users to see if anyone else is ready. The table contains the address of the user's dictionary and a flag:

ready or not? The I/O complete interrupt routines simply mark the proper user ready. And if no one is ready, the computer scans the table endlessly - it's got nothing better to do. Naturally, upon program start-up, no one is ready.

7.2 Queing

You can save yourself a lot of trouble by putting some code in the user controller. Two subroutines: QUE and UNQUE. When a user needs a facility that might be in use by someone else, he calls QUE. If it's available, he gets it. If it's not available, he joins the que of people waiting for it. When it is released, and his turn, he will get it.

For example, he can't read disk if someone else if reading disk. Or at least he can't use a particular channel or device. While he's waiting, of course he relinquishes control. When he's through with the facility, he calls UNQUE which passes it to someone else.

These are extremely valuable routines, for there are many facilities that can be handled in the manner; each disk, each line (shared lines), the printer, block 1 (disk allocation), non-re-entrant routines (SQRT). An extension will even permit exclusive use of blocks.

Naturally, I have in mind a specific way to implement QUE and UNQUE. And I caution you, more strongly than usual, that plausible modifications won't work. I'll try to mention all the reasons.

In addition to the user's dictionary address and ready flag, each user must have a link field - not in his dictionary, but in user control. Each facility that is to be protected must have associated with it 2 fields: the owner, and the first person waiting. The best arrangement is to have a table of such que-words, one for each facility. If a facility is free, its owner is 0; otherwise its owner is the number of the user owning it. A user's number is his position in the table of users, starting at 1. If no one is waiting, a facility's waiter field is 0; otherwise it is the number of the user waiting.

If I want a facility and its free:

I place my number in the owner field and exit.

If it's busy, but no one's waiting:

I place my number in the waiter field, 0 my link field, and relinquish control.

If someone's waiting:

I follow the chain of links starting at the waiter's link field until I find a 0 link; I place my number there, 0 my link field, and relinquish control.

When I'm through with a facility (UNQUE):

IF no one's waiting, I 0 the owner field, and exit.

If someone's waiting, I move his number to the owner field, move his link field to the waiter field, mark him ready, and exit.

The whole procedure is simple and efficient. It handles a lot of potential problems in a reasonable and effective way. Several comments: The queues will probably be very short. In fact, facilities will usually be free, unless the computer is over-loaded. A user can not be in more than one queue. However, a user can own more than one facility. Hence the need for a waiter field with each facility: a que must descend from each facility, and not from each owner; the two concepts are independent. You must add to the error routine a loop to release any facilities held by the current user. Since a user needs to know his own number in order to queue, this number must be stored in a field in his dictionary and be set by the re-initialize routine.

It's complicated, it's troublesome, and it's the price you must pay for multiple users.

7.2.1 Usage

To gain exclusive use of a block, with the exception of block 1, best handled as an exception, set aside some facility que-words for this purpose. Find a free one and store the block number it represents somewhere, then treat that block like any other facility. When the last waiter releases the block, release the facility que-word for re-use. Notice that this technique has no effect upon the block itself. It may be resident in core, or not.

Anyone may read or write it. However, no one else may have exclusive use of it. If all users cooperate to request exclusive use when they should, it works perfectly - with no extra cost to ordinary reads/writes. Actually, exclusive use of a block is necessary only under exceptional circumstances. Block 1 is an example of such: The block may not be used by anyone else until another block has been read, and the available space up-dated.

7.3 Private dictionaries

The key to the case of conversion to multiple users is that all required information about a user is stored in his dictionary - a single contiguous area of core. He makes extensive use of code that belongs to the system, and that does not reside in his dictionary. On the other hand, code unique to his application may reside there. Here is the first decision that you must make: What belongs in the user's private dictionary?

Let us look at the arrangement of core. If we choose, and we should, it follows dictionary format: each entry followed by the code it executes. Each entry is linked to the previous so that the dictionary may be searched backwards. Some entries are obviously of interest to all applications: those that control the stack, that define dictionary entries, that specify fields such as BASE, CONTEXT, etc. Other entries are probably of local concern: the names of fields in records, definitions used to edit text, special purpose code (random number generator, square root, etc.). At some point you must separate the system and user dictionaries.

If you establish several user dictionaries, the first entry in each will link to the system dictionary (Fig 7.1) at the same point. Thus, each user is unaware of any other user, and his dictionary search is unaffected.

7.3.1 Memory protection

If all users will fit into the core simultaneously, we are finished. You divide memory into the appropriate dictionaries. You should provide memory protection so that one user cannot damage another. The stack and dictionary size checking discussed earlier, should be augmented by checks on the = operator, so that a user cannot write outside his dictionary, or outside a block he has read. If you have hardware memory protect, you will find it difficult to take advantage of.

The user must be able to read his dictionary, the system dictionary and the block buffers; he must be able to write his dictionary and the block buffers. Several users might want to write the same block buffer; if not simultaneously, at least consecutively. If your hardware can help, it's better than any I've seen. But software protection can be made adequate - except against malicious mischief.

Although a user cannot hurt anyone else, he is certainly capable of destroying himself. Thus; you should have a system entry that will restore his dictionary to empty, with all control fields reset. Such an entry will get heavy use, for it is a simple way to start over.

If you have implemented fixed-size entries, you have no links to lead to the system dictionary. Your search routine must separately search the user's dictionary and the system dictionary, since not all users can be contiguous to the system. This should only cost a few instructions but is another reason to prefer the linked entries.

If you have multiple chains in your dictionary, each chain must jump from the user's dictionary to the system dictionary. This is only a problem when re-initializing the dictionary, and can be easily solved, by keeping a copy of the chain heads for the system dictionary.

7.3.2 Controlled access

It would appear that you want the system dictionary as large as possible to avoid redundancy. That is not necessarily the case. There are some entries that might go into the system dictionary - except that you specifically want to deny them to some users. Prime examples are the GET and DELETE entries that control disk allocation. Misuse of these words by ignorant users can badly damage data stored on disk. The best solution is to place the code in the system, without a dictionary entry.

Define a table of entry points into code of this nature. Then if a user wants to use an entry point, he must first define it, perhaps:

17 ENTRY GET 18 ENTRY RELEASE

establishing the words GET and RELEASE with the code identified in the 17th and 18th table positions. Library subroutines (FORTRAN arithmetic subroutines) might be treated similarly.

Incidentally, this illustrates a general method of protection: In addition to using a word, the user must define it correctly. Clearly you can cascade the process. The value of such protection against malicious mischief depends on secrecy, which is always the ultimate protection. However even in the absence of secrecy, it provides valuable protection against inadvertent damage.

7.4 Disk buffers

The fact that you may have several users reading disk simultaneously has no effect at all upon the disk-access subroutine. It can search the block buffers and find an available buffer without concern as to who asked for it. Of course, you must have at least as many buffers as users.

In fact, all of core not required for dictionaries might as well be devoted to block buffers, as left idle. However, if a block is being read, you should mark the buffer busy some way, so someone else will not assume it's there before it arrives. If you attempt to read a busy block, you should relinquish control and try again when you're re-started.

7.5 User swapping

So far, we've had all users resident in core. This is by far the best arrangement for handling a small number of users. The step to allowing more users than can be simultaneously resident is a small one philosophically, but can be very difficult to implement. Suppose we had room for 4 user's dictionaries in core, but we wanted to permit 40 users. Clearly, we can store all 40 user dictionaries on disk and load each one into core when he becomes active.

Providing disk I/O is substantially faster than message I/O there is not even a performance penalty associated. When a user is awaiting message I/O we write him out to disk. When he completes his message I/O we read him back into core. Naturally, we do not move him from core when he is waiting for disk I/O, since it would take unreasonably long to write him out and read him back compared to the original delay.

So far there are no problems. The problem arises as to where to read him back into. We have 4 buffers: if we load users always into the same buffer we have 4 classes of users, each of which can go into a single buffer. We are begging for delays at one buffer while another is empty.

If we are going to the trouble anyway, we should make all buffers equivalent, and load a user into whichever one is free. However, now a user's dictionary must be relocatable. That is, any references to his dictionary must be relative to its origin, which is presumably stored in an index register. This isn't too bad if we've planned from the start - way back with a single-user program - to make all dictionary references relative; it requires almost a complete re-write of the program if we did not, for all dictionary references, and they're scattered all through the program, must be indexed.

Actually, since any references to a block must be relative to the (variable) origin of the block, we aren't introducing a new problem; merely extending an old one. However, there's another complication. We now have a real distinction between our 2 dictionaries: the system dictionary is absolute, and the user dictionary is relative. Therefore, the same kind of entry must be treated differently, depending on which dictionary it is in.

For example, if we have compiled code in the parameter area, an absolute user dictionary can store the code address in the address field. However, a relative user dictionary must store the address of a routine that will, in turn, jump into the parameter field. Or else relative addresses must be distinguished from absolute addresses, perhaps by size, and treated properly.

To avoid impossible difficulties, you should be careful to write your single-user program with the following constraints:

Reserve an index register for a user pointer, the origin of the user's dictionary, andd *use* this index. That is, treat the dictionary as relative, even though you needn't.

Make all code re-entrant. At least all code within which a user might relinquish control - which turns out to be most code.

Do this if you have the slightest intention of implementing a many-user version. This violates the Basic Principle, but we're dealing with such basic issues as to be worth it.

8. Programs that think

The mystery of consciousness has intrigued philosophers for a long time. It now seems apparent that just as life is a result of complex organization, so is consciousness. It is somehow a by-product of complex interactions among data. Interactions so complex they only occur in mammalian brains.

Therefore, one way of investigating the mind is to experiment with manipulating data. The obvious way to do this is on a computer. We now have a program with capabilities previously unattainable. Why not use it in such a way as to probe the realm of 'thinking'? I don't propose that you become a psychobiologist. But you can have a lot of fun and do some really impressive things with simple extensions to your program.

I will describe a number of entries of unusual capability. If you have an application that can use them, or if you can create an application to use them, by all means give them a try. However, the Basic Principle forbids you including them without a purpose. They are sufficiently elaborate and sufficiently specialized as to never prove unexpectedly valuable.

I have had all the entries I describe in a single program. This program had less than 1500 instructions, so it is practical to include everything in a single program. But I was experimenting, and never found an application that needed a fraction of them.

8.1 Word dissection

One of the most awkward characteristics of our program is that words must be separated by spaces. Very often you'd like to suffix punctuation or operator without an intervening space. And we will soon add abilities that make prefixing desirable, too.

It is not difficult to modify the word subroutine to recognise characters other than space as terminating characters. But it is impossible to provide satisfying generality. Inevitably, you complicate the word subroutine unduely by considering innumerable special cases. And you can waste much ingenuity trying to achieve generality.

For example, there are no simple rules that permit all these to be words:

`HELLO GOOD-BY 3.14 I.B.M. -.5 1.E-3`

Likewise, there are no simple rules that separate these strings into the words intended:

`-ALPHA 1+ ALPHA+BETA +X**-3 X,Y,Z; X.OR.Y`

But don't dispair! There is a general solution that can handle all these cases. It is expensive in time, perhaps very expensive. But it solves the problem so thoroughly, while demonstrating that no lesser solution is possible, that I consider it well worth the price. Besides, the speed of processing text is not a critical factor. We maximize speed precisely so that we can afford extravagances such as this.

If you haven't already guessed: We read a word terminated by a space, search the dictionary, and convert it to a number. If it isn't a word by this definition, we drop the last character and try again. Eventually we strip off enough characters so that the remainder is a word.

Let me review the cost. We do as many dictionary searches (plus numeric conversions) as there are letters to be dropped. This encourages fast searches and quick recognition of non-numbers. It also encourages minimizing the length of strings that must be dissected. But let's be practical: The number of occassions when dissection is convenient are few enough that you can afford the price. With the exception of compiler source code. But I'm not writing a compiler, and if you are you can probably make your word subroutine cope.

There are several things to be careful of: As you drop characters from the aligned word, you must keep track of your current position within this word. However, you must also back-up the input pointer so that you can start the next word correctly. Incidently this requires an initial back-up over the terminal space that is not repeated.

Backing the input pointer is not possible with unbuffered input. This is why I suggested that you buffer un-buffered devices back in Chapter 3. If you aren't going to dissect, apply the Basic Principle.

You must also have a way to detect that you have dropped the last character: a counter is one solution. Another is to place a space immediately ahead of your aligned word, and to stop on the space. I prefer the second, for I find I lack a convenient counter that is preserved over dictionary search and numeric conversion. But this means that I must fetch each character before I deposit a space over it. And this means that my fetch subroutine must operate backwards, the only place I ever need to fetch backwards. It depends on your hardware.

There are 2 things we can do to refine this dissection. They are incompatible, and the choice depends on your application: We don't need to drop characters one-at-a-time. If you have several letters in succession, or several digits, or perhaps a combination, you might drop them all and then perform a single search/conversion. This means that you must examine each character (which suggests the second termination above). It also means that you must be able to distinguish alphanumerics from special-characters. This requires a 64-character table of character type tailored to your particular character set and application. If your hardware permits, you may be able to use a 64-bit table - classic trade-off of time vs. space.

However, this means you cannot dissect letter strings and you might want to. Plurals, for instance, can be easily accommodated by dropping the terminal 's'. On the other hand, you can easily mis-identify words by dissecting letter strings: I once dissected the word SWAP: S was defined, W was defined and my error message was AP ? . Perhaps when dropping a single letter, you should replace it with a dash to indicate a word stem. Or perhaps it doesn't matter if unidentifiable words are mis-identified.

One further caution: If you are going to dissect, you must not discard extra characters while initially aligning the word. Your input pointer must be positioned so that you can backspace it correctly. If you exceed maximum word size, stop immediately and supply a terminal space. This means that no single word can exceed maximum size, which has now become maximum string size.

Another optimization has to do with the size of words in the dictionary. If you only match part of the word, you may as well start dropping characters at that point, if number format permits.

What does word dissection mean to a program? How does it help it 'think'? It means that your program can read your mind. It means that no matter how you type something, the computer will extract the meaning you intended. It will use the meaning of the longest character string it can, consistent with a left-to-right scan. It's not infallible: if you define +1 and then type +1000 it will misunderstand. But if you use your language consistently, it will follow.

I would like to be able to say that this ability will impress people. It will impress you - at least it should. But ordinary people, like your boss, expect this kind of ability from computers. They are only impressed, negatively, if they discover its absence.

8.2 Level definitions

I am embarrassed not to know the standard terminology for what I am going to discuss. I have never heard it discussed and I have never searched for it. But it must be a standard aspect of compiler writing - discussed in courses dealing with compilers. If you know the terminology, you also know most of what I'm going to say: although I hope I can get you to stretch its application.

Our arithmetic operators have found their arguments already on the stack. Conventional algebraic notation uses such operators as infixes, and a left-right scan provides only 1 operand when the operator is discovered. Consequently, the operation must be deferred until the other operand is available.

Moreover, we have a hierarchy of operations than control when that other operator becomes available. For example:

A+B*C

the multiply must be done before the add. Moreover, parentheses are used to modify the standard hierarchy:

A*(B+C)

Such a notation is completely equivalent to ours. It offers no advantages over the operands-preceding-operator and has some limitations. But people are accustomed to it and negatively-impressed by its absence. So, I will show you how to provide the capability.

However, there is no reason to restrict our attention to the customary arithmetic and/or logical operators. I will show you some other similar hierarchies. The capability I describe will handle them all.

Let us establish a new kind of dictionary entry. It is identical to a definition except that it has a number appended, a level number. So, let's call it a level-definition. The rule is that a level-definition is not to be executed when it is encountered, but rather placed on a push-down stack. It will be executed when another definition with a equal or smaller level number is encountered.

A convenient format for level-definitions is:

2 :L word . . . ;

The 2 is the level number, taken from the stack. :L declares the next word as a level-definition. ';' marks the end.

Let's talk about + and *:

0 :L , ;

1 :L + + ;

2 :L * * ;

We have re-defined them in terms of their old definitions, but as level-definitions. We defined ',' to have some way to stop. Now we can say:

3 + 4 * 5 ,

What happened? 3 goes onto the parameter stack, + goes onto the level-stack, 4 onto the parameter stack, * onto the level-stack (since it has a higher-level number than the + already there), 5 onto the parameter stack. Now ',' forces the * to be executed (since its level number is smaller) and * finds 5 and 4 on the parameter stack. ',' also forces + to be executed (with arguments 20 and 3) and then, because its level number is 0, is itself executed and does nothing.

Clear? I would like to assume you're familiar with this technique, but I don't quite dare. All I'm really contributing is a way to implement with dictionary entries a technique usually built into compilers. Perhaps the cop-out of suggesting you define the arithmetic operators and work out some examples for yourself. Remember that *equal* level operators force each other out, and that a *lower* level operator forces out a higher. It is strangely easy to reason out the relative levels of operators incorrectly.

What do we have so far? Why should you be interested in level-definitions? You've seen a couple, their definitions are simple. Level-definitions tend to be simple compared to ordinary definitions. But given level-definitions you can write a compiler, for any language! Level-definitions are necessary and sufficient to implement any context-free grammar, not only the LR-1 grammars at the base of contemporary languages. Frankly I don't know what to do with the power they provide, but I'll toss out some suggestions later.

Now back to work. You've seen some level definitions. I hope you've played with them some. How do we implement them? Well we don't. Rather we implement a generalization: level-entries. When I found an application for level-entries I also found out it was cheaper to implement level-definitions as such than the way I was doing.

Every dictionary entry may be considered a virtual-computer instruction, as discussed in Chapter 5. We consider a level-entry an instruction whose execution can be delayed - after the fashion of a level definition. Why not? A definition is, after all, only a particular sort of instruction. If it may be profitably delayed, so might other instructions.

I'm sorry if it seems complicated. It is! It's going to get more complicated - you aren't getting something for nothing. But it's worth it. However, notice that everything we're doing now builds on everything we've done before. Notice that the concept of a special sort of entry depends on having a dictionary available; and the extension of definitions to include level numbers depends on having definitions. We are gradually building a tree and are in the higher branches. We might not depend on all the lower branches, but we have to have some.

How do you execute a level-entry? Exactly the same as any other. However, the first thing the level-entry does is execute the LEVEL routine, to give it a name, with its level number as parameter. LEVEL tests this level number against the level-stack. 3 cases arise:

It may place the level number and entry on the level-stack (higher level entry) and RETURN.

It may replace the top of the level-stack with this entry, and execute the old top.

If the level-stack is empty, and the level is 0, it will execute this entry.

All 3 cases are required!

Before actually executing an entry from the stack, LEVEL must set the SOURCE address to reference another routine, FORCE. You recall that your main control loop obtains its next entry either by reading a word and searching, or by fetching from a definition. Well here is a third source, the level-stack. As for a definition, the old value of SOURCE and the virtual-IC must be saved - on the return-stack.

When you finally force execution of a level-entry, you must remember that it has already been executed, and immediately jump to LEVEL. This re-execution must start at a different place, 1 or 2 instructions below the routine address, perhaps. Or you might include the re-start address as a parameter and keep it in the level-stack.

When a level-entry is done, it will RETURN, and your control loop will go to FORCE. The only way you can get to FORCE is by completing a level-entry. Its function is to check the level stack and see if any other entry can be forced off by the one on top. 3 cases arise:

It may leave the level-stack alone (higher level on top) and restore SOURCE and virtual-IC from return-stack, and RETURN.

It may execute the lower entry, replacing it with the top - thus dropping the level-stack.

If there is no lower entry, and the level is 0, it will execute the top entry - thus emptying the level-stack. At this time, it will restore from the return-stack.

Let me emphasize the importance of the return-stack, and the necessity of saving SOURCE. If a level-entry is in fact a definition, SOURCE will be reset yet again. It may be some time before we return and encounter FORCE once again. For in fact, a level-definition may occur within a definition; and it may execute other definitions - indeed, other level definitions. The whole process may become incomprehensibly enmeshed, and indeed it does in practice. But it will sort itself out. The beauty of definitions, level-definitions particularly, is similar to that of recursive functions. You need consider only the simple case when making the definition; complex cases take care of themselves.

Now you should be able to implement level-entries, definitions among them. What can you do with them?

You can define the customary arithmetic operations: + - * / MOD **.

You can define the customary logical operations: OR AND NOT IMPL.

You can define infix relations: = < > <= >= /=.

You can define an infix replacement: = := (one that works in either direction).

You can define all the above.

It depends on your application.

You can define words like PLUS MINUS TIMES DIVIDED-BY EQUALS; an English language arithmetic.

You can define phrases like MOVE . . TO . . or DIVIDE . . INTO . . or ADD . . TO . . A COBOL language arithmetic.

But let me mention 2 particular uses:

Consider a statement with the form
   IF relation THEN statement ELSE statement ;

Define IF so it will be forced out by THEN and generate a conditional branch. Define THEN so it will be forced out by ELSE and fix-up the adddress left dangling by IF. Define ELSE so it will first generate an unconditional branch, then force out THEN, and then await being forced out itself. Define ; to force out ELSE and fix-up the forward branch.

With a few statements you can implement any such compiler construct.

Consider a statement like

   1800. FT / SEC ** 2

Define a kind of entry UNIT that puts a constant on the stack immediately and acts like a multiply when it's forced to. Define / to put a 1. on to the stack immediately and divide when it's forced to. Define ** as an infix, and FT and SEC as UNITs.

This expression and any others you construct will be evaluated correctly.

I pass the ball to you. If you have an application that could profit from a natural language input format, you have the capability with level definitions to implement it. For example, it would not be hard to teach your program to solve the problems at the end of a high-school physics text.

Keep in mind, that level-entries do not enhance the power of the computer. They merely let you specify instructons in what, to the computer, is an unnatural order. You are well advised to get your application working, and *then* to append a fancy control language.

How does this relate to a program 'thinking'? Solely by deferring to the human-oriented format of control languages. Not even this is impressive to anyone but us! And even how impressed are you by FORTRAN's expression evaluator any longer?

8.3 Infinite dictionary

I would guess that your dictionary will average several hundred entries. Even a small amount of data seems to generate a large number of fields - to mention one source. However, some applications need much larger vocabularies. Perhaps you need to identify one of 10,000 customers; or maybe you want the symbols for 104 elements available; or the names of 1000 approved additives.

Clearly such volume must be stored on disk. Also, clearly, you don't want to have to search disk explicitly. There is a gratifyingly effective solution: If you can't find the word in the core dictionary, and it's not a number, search a block on disk. Now the question reduces to: Which block?

Establish a field called CONTEXT. Treat it like you did a block address: it both identifies a block and suggests where it might be in core. Search this block. By changing CONTEXT you can search different disk dictionaries. By linking several blocks together, you can search larger amounts of disk; or search several dictionaries in sequence.

You can afford to search a fair amount of disk, because if you can't find the word you're going to generate an error message. A delay in typing that message to make sure you can't find the word, is an excellent investment. Still for really large vocabularies - thousands of entries - such an approach is inadequate.

For very large dictionaries, scramble the word into a block address and search that block. By that I mean compute a block address from the letters in a word, just as we did for multiple chains in the core dictionary, though you'll probably want a different algorithm. You can search one of a thousand blocks and be assured that if the word is anywhere, it's in that block. Because you used the same scramble technique to put it there as you use to find it. Since many words will scramble into the same block, you of course search for an exact match. Again, just as in core.

With such a large disk dictionary, you want to be careful of several things. First, once you choose a scrambling algorithm you can never change it; so make a good choice before you define lots of entries. Second, try to keep the number of entries roughly the same in all blocks; and roughly equal to half the capacity of a block - to compensate for the first "roughly". Or else provide for overflow by linking blocks together.

Such a disk dictionary can be really impressive - even to non-computer folk - because you have fast access to a prodigous vocabulary. Fast means you can search tens-of-thousands of entries in a single disk access.

What do disk dictionary entries look like? I have found that 2 fields are sufficient: the word field, the same size as the core dictionary word field; and a parameter field, 1 word long. If you find a match on disk, you put the parameter on the stack. Remember that you can't afford to store absolute addresses on disk, so you can't have an address field as in core. You could provide a coded address field, but it seems adequate to treat disk entries as constants.

For instance, you can name blocks. When you type the name of a block its address is moved from the parameter field onto the stack. That is an excellent place for it, because if you type the block number itself that's where it would be placed. You can use block numbers and block names interchangeably. Thus, when you type an account number the block associated with that account is placed onto the stack, whereupon you store it into the base word that its fields reference. An illegal account will cause an error message, in the ordinary way. Or you might name the instructions for your computer. Then typing its name will place a 1-word instruction on the stack, ready for further processing.

Although I spoke of account numbers, notice that you can't number blocks. That is, the name of a disk dictionary entry cannot be a number. For if you type a number it will be converted onto the stack, and never sought on disk. And you must attempt to convert *before* searching disk or you'll search disk for every literal you type. But then "numbers" often don't look much like the numbers defined by NUMBER. They tend to have embedded dashes, letters and such; or else you can prefix a letter or suffix a # character.

How do you put an entry on disk? A special defining entry:

0 **NAME ZERO**

analogous to CONSTANT. Alternatively, you might set a flag and let the dictionary entry subroutine decide whether to use disk or core. This latter is preferable if you have several dfferent kinds of entries that might go either to disk or core.

You will also need a way to forget disk entries:

FORGET ZERO

FORGET must call WORD as defining entries do, since this is a non-typical use of the word ZERO. When it finds the entry, it simple clears it without trying to pack. Your entry routine should first search disk to see if the word is already there. You don't want multiple definitions on disk, even though there're useful in core. Then it should search for a hole. If it finds the word already there, or if it can't find a hole? You guessed it, an error message.

Let's talk about a refinement. With a thousand names on disk it's easy to run out of mnemonics. Let's re-use the field CONTEXT: after you scramble the word into a block address, add the contents of CONTEXT and search that block. If CONTEXT is 0, no difference. But if CONTEXT is non-zero, you're searching a different block. If CONTEXT can vary from 0 to 15, you can have 16 different definitions of the same word. You'll find the one that had the same value of CONTEXT when you defined it. If there is no entry for a word under a given CONTEXT, you won't get a match. A block containing a definition for the same word under a different CONTEXT won't be searched.

For example, stock numbers might look the same for different sales-lines. By setting CONTEXT you can distinguish them. You can use the same name for a report screen that you use for its instruction screen; distinguish them by CONTEXT. If you're scrambling anyway, you may as well add in CONTEXT (modulo a power of 2); it costs nothing, and vastly extends the universe of names. In fact, you can use CONTEXT in both the ways we've discussed, simultaneously. For as an aditive constant it tends to be small; and as a block number, large. So, your search routine can decide whether to scramble or not based on its size.

A problem arises if you plan to dissect words. All those extra dictionary searches are augmented by disk searches and their attendant disk accesses. Several solutions are possible: Scramble with only the first couple of characters, so at least the disk searches are in the same block - which will be in core. Or use only non-zero values of CONTEXT and let 0 inhibit the disk search. That is, make dissection and disk searching mutually exclusive. As is often the case, the problem is serious only if you aren't aware of it.

8.4 Infinite memory

Of course, you can't really have infinite memory. Not even unlimited memory. But you can access directly the entire random memory available to your computer. A small augmentation of the field entries introduced in Chapter 4 will do it. I postponed the discussion to here because it has no particular connection with output, and because it's impressive enough to relate to 'thinking'.

The problem of what to do with infinite memory, I leave up to you. You will have to organize it somehow. Examine different parts of it, move fields around, what you will. All I can do is show you how to eliminate any explicit reference to disk.

Let's include in our field a parameter that points to a disk address. The field is assumed to be relative to that address; that is, contained in the disk block. The program will automatically read the block to obtain the field. Of course, a number of fields will point to the same block address.

Before you start objecting, let me rush on. Stored with the block address is the location of the core buffer that block last occuppied. So the program needn't actually read disk, or even search core buffers for the block, unless the block has been overlaid. Hence repeated accesses to the same block cost little.

Several trade-offs are involved: You should have a generous number of core buffers to minimize overlays. You should choose you block size with this use in mind. Accessing such disk-resident fields is slower than if you deliberately read the block into a fixed location and access it there; but the ease with which you can address data scattered on disk, and the beauty of being able to forget that some data is on disk and other data in core, to me make up for the loss in speed. Besides, it's your problem to implement the feature in a way that is efficient.

Suppose you want to scan a portion of disk. All you have to do is define the fields and establish a loop: start with the first block address, store it in the base location where the fields expect it and increment it each time through the loop. All right, your advantage is marginal. All you save is a read instruction. But if that block links to another one, all you need do is store the link in the base location for other fields and forget that a link is involved. If you access fields in the link it will automatically be read. If not, it won't be. The more complex your data, the greater the advantage.

Of course, you don't have to worry about writing blocks either. Chapter 6 talked about flagging blocks that need writing, rather than writing them immediately. Pays off here! If you change a field, its block will be re-written; if you don't, it won't. Just make sure that when you say GOOD-BY your program writes all changed blocks.

You can make these field entries identical with those accessing core, by making the pointer to the base address 0. If you don't point to a disk address, you must mean core.

Notice that this addition of a base to a field entry defines a data structure very much like the levels in COBOL's data division: 01 level corresponding to the disk address; 02 levels to the fields themselves. For a few extra instructions you can add higher levels: If the pointer does not reference a disk address, but another field description, you have the equivalent of 03 level, etc.

Consider how the field reference actually works. In the field entry you have a word parameter that tells which word the field is in (or starts in). If this field references another, you add the word parameters together. When you find the core address of the disk block, you add the word offset and voila': you have the word you want. Going through intermediate fields has little advangage unless the intermediate fields change. Why not? By incrementing a base field address, you can access different rows of a matrix or different records in a block. Or you can access different sub-records of a record. Very useful! It's enough to make me think COBOL is a pretty good language. Of course, you can do the same thing with core fields, you just never point to a disk address at the very end.

A word of warning! Don't try to gain efficiency by putting the core address of a block in an index register. It's too hard to keep track of which block, if any, the index is currently identifying. You simply have to go through a fair bit of code to provide useful generality. Of course, your hardware might have some special features: maybe microprogramming? Even indirect addressing might be helpful.

Given such elaborate addressing capabilities, you can use some help debugging your screens. Memory protection is easy to provide, and very helpful. Include with each field entry a maximum size (in words) for that field. When you calculate an address that purports to be in that field, make sure it is. The upper limit for the final block reference is of course the block size. The upper limit for a core reference is also known. A simple error message stating OVERFLOW will catch trouble before it has a chance to propagate.

You might want to implement an additional kind of field entry. This one has a link. If you make a reference that lies outside the field, it will follow this link and attempt to satisfy your request. In particular, a record entry that points to a block: If you increment the record offset beyond the end of the block, you can pick up a link from the block, change the block address, reset the record offset and access the new, overflow block. Automatically! This makes for a very attractive implementation of variable length records (actually blocks), providing the records are composed of fixed-length pieces.

If you want such an overflow capability, you must provide a way of constructing the links. You need an entry that will search a block (chain) for a record-size hole - of course all holes are the same size. If you can't find a hold, you must GET a new block, link it, and then you have a block full of holes. A hole should be identified by a 0 in the first word, character or bit, so that when GET clears the new block to 0, all record positions are empty. Naturally you have no guarantee that overflow blocks will be near each other. Almost certainly they won't be. Either you don't care, or you initially allocate each block chain sequentially, up to mean size.

It is easy to remove a record. You create a hole by storing 0 in the first word. It is hard to discover whether by doing this you have caused an empty block which can be un-chained. Unless you expect your data to shrink and need to recover space, don't bother. How can data shrink? Also, don't move records around - to squeeze out holes perhaps. Just as we want to use absolute block addresses, we want to use absolute record addresses (if we use record addresses at all).

So, we can have automatic access to fields scattered all over disk and in variable size records at that. Basic Principle!

One thing! If field entries can address other field entries, you need some way to distinguish a field from a disk address. I have no suggestion.

9. Programs that bootstrap

It is sometimes hard to appreciate how it all gets started. We have been tacitly assuming that your computer has a compiler and that you used it to compile your program. But how did your compiler get written? Today the answer is certainly that it was prepared by another compiler on another computer. We've achieved parity with the biological maxim: all life comes from previously existing life. For practical purposes, all programs are prepared by previously existing programs.

Although this makes life somewhat easier for compiler writers, especially when the target computer isn't built yet, it has a drawback. You can never drop your ultimate dependence on the pre-existing program. If you use a compiler that generates certain instructions, or assumes a certain disk format, you are constrained to be compatible. Consider that a simple version of our program, providing it includes compiler verbs, is perfectly capable of compiling itself. It can do this with greater freedom than the standard compiler, but more important, you can then discard the standard compiler.

In Chapter 1, I discussed the sad state of software quality. Although we can prepare an excellent object program, we are obliged to maintain it as a source program for an unhappy compromise of a compiler. I must admit that this is the most expedient way to get the program started. However, I question whether it is most efficient over the long haul of re-compiling and modifying.

Let us imagine a situation in which you have access to your computer. I mean sole user sitting at the board with all the lights, for some hours at a time. This is admittedly an a-typical situation, but one that can always be arranged if you are competent, press hard, and will work odd hours. Can you and the computer write a program? Can you write a program that didn't descend from a pre-existing program? You can learn a bit and have a lot of fun trying.

9.1 Getting started

First, you'll have to know some things: how to turn the computer on and off (odd hours), how to enter and display data from the console switches, and how to avoid damaging data stored on disk. You may have to corner operators or engineers to discover such information; it is so rarely of interest it doesn't get written down.

So now you're face to face with the computer. What do you do? First an exercise. Initialize the interrupt locations in such a way that the computer will run, will execute an endless loop, when you start it. OK? Then modify your loop so that it will clear memory. OK? You've probably learned a lot.

Now we're going to start for real. We're going to start building your dictionary, even though you can't use it yet. You must choose your entry format now; variable-sized entries are required, but you can decide about word-size and layout. The first entry is SAVE; it will save your program on disk. Lacking a control loop you'll have to jump to it manually, but at least you can minimize re-doing a lot of work. The second entry is LOAD; it will re-load your program from disk. You may have a hardware load button, if you can store your program compatibly with it, fine. You might want to punch a load card, to provide initial load otherwise. But it's always convenient to be able to re-start from core.

The third entry is DUMP; it will dump core onto the printer. It needn't be very fast to be a lot faster than looking with the switches. This probably isn't a trivial routine, but it oughtn't take more than a dozen instructions. You might want to postpone it just a bit.

So, with a couple hours work - providing you read the manual first - you have an operating system (SAVE, LOAD) and debugging package (DUMP). And you know a lot about your computer.

9.2   The roots

Lest you worry, I have gone through this process myself. I've done it twice, actually, and I'm not describing it as I did it, but as I now think I should have done it. So you've room for improvisation.

In a sense we're building a tree. We've now reached a point where we can start making the roots. For a while everything will be concealed but we'll eventually reach daylight and start on branches.

I presume you can LOAD your program and DUMP core. It's time to get away from the switches and use the typewriter. So, set up a message buffer from which you can send and receive text. Presumably when awaiting text your program sits in an endless loop somewhere. Learn to recognise that loop. You'll spend most of your running time there and it's reassuring to know that everything's all right.

No dictionary entry is associated with message I/O. You could define one, but we won't need it. In general, we will construct entries only when they'll be needed. We can always add any entry we need, later.

You're doing great. Now establish the stacks, the dictionary search subroutine and entries for WORD and NUMBER. Be very careful to do it right the first time; that is, don't simplify NUMBER and plan to re-do it later. The total amount of work is greater, even using the switches.

Now write a control loop. You might test the stack but jump to an unspecified error routine. And run. DUMP is still our only output routine, but you should be able to read and execute words like DUMP, SAVE and LOAD.

Write an entry for ENTRY, the subroutine that constructs dictionary entries. I haven't specified the code executed for WORD, NUMBER and ENTRY. These are subroutines, and the only time we'll use their names is when compiling code. So, they should execute code that generates a call instruction. We haven't written that code yet. Now define the code-entry, the word that names code; and the deposit word, the word that places the stack in core. Now you can type octal numbers and store them in the dictionary. No more switches. You can also construct new dictionary entries, for code.

9.3 The branches

We've reached a milestone. The invisible work is done, and we can have a written record of what remains. There are many things to do and the order not so obvious. We've reached the position of having a source language, and we need to be able to modify it and re-compile without re-doing everything. Here we're forced to generate temporary code that will become obsolete, but it will save a lot of effort.

First a READ and WRITE entry to provide disk-access to a single core buffer. Then a simple T and R to type and replace lines of text in that block. These entries will later become obsolete, so keep them simple.

We now need the READ and ;S verbs for screens. Specify a block number and we can read the text in that block.

Now we write screens that provide definitions, an improved compiler, improved block handler, improved text-editor and we can proceed with our application. We want a REMEMBER entry. We haven't needed it so far bacause we could always reach in and reset the dictionary manually.

I'm sure you've noticed the difficulty with modifying code in the root. A powerful tool is to be able to shift the dictionary in core. If the root doesn't use absolute addresses, define a SHIFT entry and use it. Otherwise minimize the number of absolute addresses and define a more elaborate SHIFT verb that adjusts them.

Be careful SAVEing your program. Keep a back-up of your old version before SAVEing a new one, just in case.

####

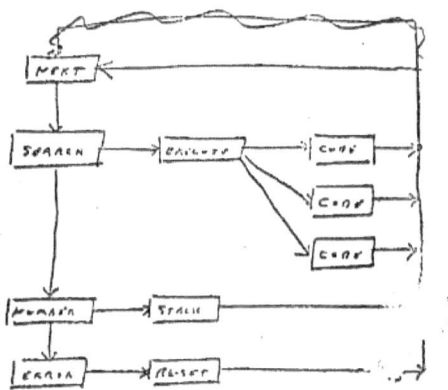

FIG. 1, CONTROL PROGRAM

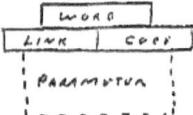

FIG 2 DICTIONARY ENTRY

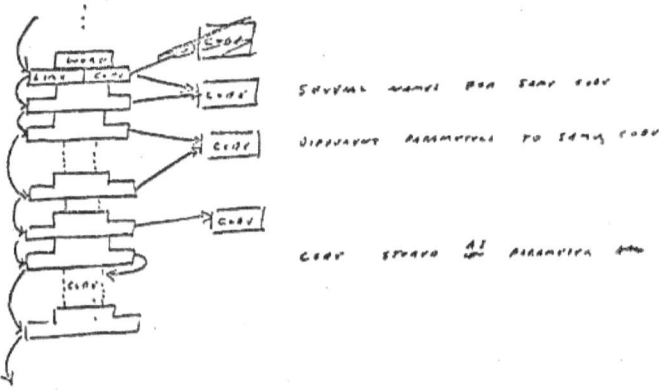

FIG 3 PORTION OF DICTIONARY

Figure 6.2

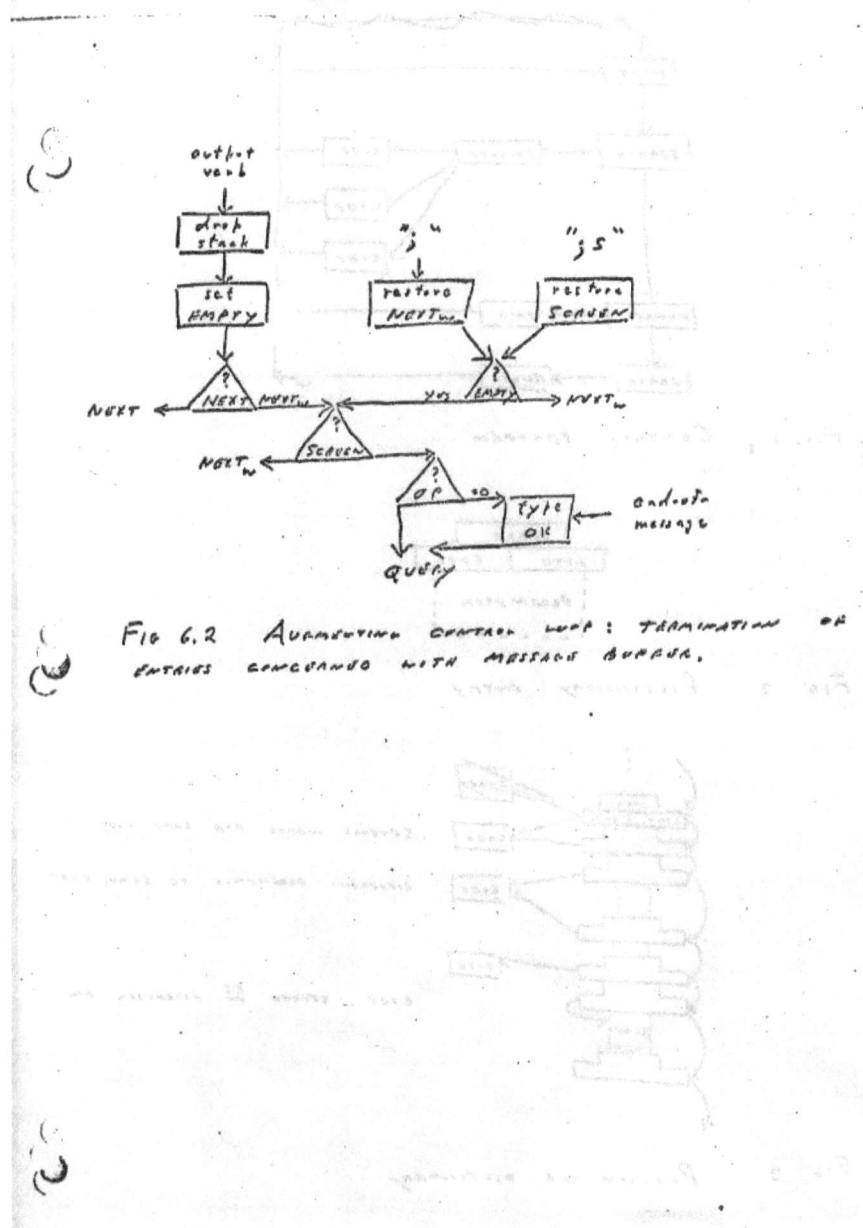

FIG 6.2 AUGMENTING CONTROL LOOP: TERMINATION OF ENTRIES CONCURRING WITH MESSAGE BUFFER.

www.ingramcontent.com/pod-product-compliance
Lightning Source LLC
Chambersburg PA
CBHW020657220526
45464CB00001B/467